OPTIONS TRADING:

A BEGINNER'S GUIDE TO

INVESTING IN OPTIONS

Learn How To Day Trade For Income,
Dominate Techniques, Strategies And
Trading Psychology And Start Living In
The Financial Independence Zone

MARK KRATTER

Table of Contents

Introduction

If you have spent any time looking at the world of investing, you may have heard about options at one point or another. They are sometimes going to seem pretty overwhelming to think about, but if you know a few key points that come with them, options can be pretty easy to understand. Options can be seen as another class of assets, just like mutual funds, ETFs, bonds, and stocks. And when the investor properly uses them, they can offer you some unique advantages that trading with the other assets just can't. You can purchase options like most other asset classes, simply by using an investment account from a brokerage. You may want to do a bit of research with these ahead of time to ensure you find the right brokerage firm for your needs. Options can be a powerful tool because they are going to do some wonders when it comes to enhancing your portfolio.

Options can provide you with this advantage as the offer a source of additional income, greater protection and further leverage. Based on the situation, you will find some sort of options contract that can provide you with an adequate alternative. In turbulent times, options are a great means of protecting your portfolio against sharp and unexpected declines.

In addition to protecting some of your personal assets, options are sometimes used to generate a recurring income. And some investors will choose to use these in a more speculative purpose, such as wagering on the direction that a stock will take. Just like with any of the other choices that you make with investing, options will involve some risks and you must fully understand these and know how to avoid them as much as possible. This is why any time you want to start trading options with a broker, there is going to be some kind of disclaimer like the following to help you know about the risk with options: Options involve risks and are not suitable for everyone. Options trading can be speculative in nature and carry substantial risk of loss. Only invest in risk capital. Options are going to belong to a larger group of securities that are known as derivatives. This is a word that many investors are going to associate with excessive risk-taking. In the past, Warren Buffett has even referred to these derivatives as a weapon of mass destruction when it comes to the stock market.

While there is some truth to this assertion, particularly when it comes to the irresponsible use of derivatives, the fact is that most derivatives are a good way for smaller investors to make some tidy profits. However, it is important to be aware that a derivative is a financial instrument that is based on the value on what is known as an "underlying asset". This means that the valuation of the contact will depend on the valuation of the asset that it is tied to. It should also be noted that you never actually own the asset when you take out an option until that option is exercised. By the same token, you never actually sell the asset until the option goes through.

CHAPTER 1:

Options: The Basics

What is an Option?

An option is basically an agreement on the underlying shares of stock. It's an agreement to exchange shares at a fixed price over a certain timeframe (they can be bought or sold). The first thing that you should understand about options is the following. Why would someone get involved with the options trading in the first place? Most people come to options trading with the hope of earning profits from trading the options themselves. And that's probably going to describe most readers of this book. But to truly understand what you're doing, you need to understand why options exist, to begin with.

There are probably three main reasons that options on stocks exist. The first reason is that it allows people that have shares of stock to earn money from their investment in the form of regular income. So, it can be an alternative to dividend income or even enhance dividend income. As we are going to see you later, if you own a minimum of 100 shares of some stock, this is a possibility. Then you can sell options against the stock and earn income from that over time intervals lasting from a week to a month, generally speaking. Obviously, such a move entails some risk, but people will enter positions of that type when the relative risk is low.

The second reason that people get involved with options is that they offer insurance against a collapse of the stock. So, once again, an option involves being able to trade shares of the stock at a fixed price that is set at the time the contract is originated. One type of contract allows the buyer to purchase shares, the other allows the buyer to sell shares. This allows people who own large numbers of shares to purchase something that provides protection of their investment that would allow them to sell the shares at a fixed price, in the event that their stock was declining by huge amounts on the market. So, the concept is exactly like paying insurance premiums. It's unclear how many people actually use this in practice, but this is one of the reasons that options exist. The way this would work would be that you pay someone a premium to secure the right to sell them your stock at a fixed price over some time frame. Then if the share price drops well below that degree to price, you would still be able to sell your shares and avoid huge losses that were occurring on the market.

The third reason that I would give for the existence of options is that it provides a way for people to make arrangements to purchase shares of stock at the prices that they find attractive, which aren't necessarily available on the market. So, there is a degree of speculation here. But let's just say that a particular stock you are interested in is trading at $100 a share. Furthermore, let's assume that people are extremely bullish on the stock and they are expecting it to rise by a great deal in the coming weeks. Maybe, it's earnings season.

During earnings season, stock can move by huge amounts. But before the earnings call, nobody knows whether the stock is going to go up or down or by how much it's going to move. An options contract could allow someone to speculate and set up a situation where they could profit from a huge move upward without having to actually invest in the stock.

Advantages of Option Trading

Option trading has many advantages for investors. Essentially, it is an investment that offers an opportunity for those who have the capital to delve into an income generation venture. Advantages with options trading are multiple and should motivate people into the sector of trading securities, selling and buying assets as well as earning interests that accrue.

First is the ability of this venture to aid to manage risks when investing in stocks and securities. They can cushion one from having to incur losses in investment. This is because investing in the stocks and shares usually involves risks of all in the value of the shares. This devaluation can lead to a dwindling of the profits and may, in fact, cut into the shares that one holds. However, the options marketing ensure that one is hedged from such uncertainty and as well as guarantees that a person can earn value from the trading of the shares.

Options trading is also advantageous is it allows someone the time to decide about purchase or not. This is particularly the advantage of the call options. The contract usually has a period during which a person considers the exercise of the implied rights. The person studies the market and its performance and has the allowance to understand his financial situation before making a decision on whether to purchase the shares or not. This leads one to make decisions about investments that are reasoned out. It always comes with more preparedness to handle the consequences of the decisions that one takes. This helps to rid the habit of making trading decisions on whims that can later lead to anxiety and worry as market forces swing into play.

Leverage

Leverage is a very advantageous aspect of options trading that people try to take advantage of and participate in the security market. In leverage, one has to place smaller outlays with a prospect of making higher profits in view. This encourages those who do not have the capital to invest in the underlying assets or shares to find a way of investing and get returns. One of the important parts of leverage is that one is usually getting back returns from the underlying assets or shares, yet they have not been required to pay the full cost for the purchase of the shares.

In the idea of leverage also is also the advantage of diversification. This by creating a portfolio without incurring huge initial outlays. This diversification can then create a stream of investment channels that in practice, lead to profits increasing one's earnings. Sometimes this income can increase to go above one's dividends when one takes call options that are laid again the shares owned. This extra income can even emanate from the shares that are integrated having been acquired from a lending facility. Option premiums also come ahead of the trading activities and hence cushioning one from any chances of loss.

What is an Option Contract?

When you decide to work with an options contract, you will be afforded a number of rights to go along with it. Each contract that you decide to work with will provide you with details of the following:

The type of option that you are working with. This would be a call option or a put option.

The underlying security is in the option.

The nice thing about working with options is that you can choose whether to execute them or not, so you can reduce the risk of working with them a little bit. If the market doesn't behave in the manner that you wanted it to, you simply let the expiration date go by and do nothing. You will lose out on the initial deposit that is there, but you will not lose as much money as you would have if forced to execute a bad option.

When it comes to day trading, you will find that the expiration date of the option needs to be small. You still must finish up both the purchase and the sale of the option and its underlying asset within the same day, even though options for other trading strategies can go for days, weeks, and even months. Make sure to pick out an expiration date that fits with the day trading you are doing.

Components of an Option Contract

There are various standardized components of option contracting that enable ease in engaging in options trading. These components characterize the mechanics of how options trading binds the parties involved and demonstrates the ay profits can be generated if the market forces are favorable. Among the components of options trading are:

- Underlying securities

- Contract size

- Expiry day

- Exercise prices

Underlying securities

Options that are traded on the market only apply to certain assets. These assets are then referred to as underlying securities. The word shares can be replaced with the word shares in certain instances. There are companies that provide the asset against which the option operators list options. ASX is one operator in the options trading market has played a key role in the listing of underlying securities.

The term classes of options refer to the listing of puts and calls as options of the same assets. As an example, is when puts and calls are applied to a lease corporation's shares. This does not put in regard the contract terms in terms of the predetermined price or duration of expiry of the call and put contracts. An operator of options trading usually provides the list of the available classes for the benefit of investors.

Contract Size

On the ASX platform of options trading, the market standardizes the size of the option contract at 100 underlying securities. One option contract, therefore, corresponds to 100 underlying shares. The changes that can happen only come when reorganization happens on the initial outlay of the underlying share or the capital therein. Index options usually fix the value of the contract at a certain stipulated dollar rate.

Expiry day

Options are constrained by time and have a life span. There are predetermined expiry deadlines that the platform operator sets which have to be respected. These deadlines are usually rigid, and once they are out the rights under a contract in a particular class of unexercised options are then forfeited. Usually, the last day of the life span of a contract is the summative trading date. For shares that have their expiry coming by June of 2020, the options over them have their last trading day on a Thursday that comes before the last Friday that happens to be in the month. Those that expire beyond June 2020, expiry is on the third Thursday that happens to be in the month. For index options. Expiries come on the concurrent third Thursday of the same month of writing the option. However, these dates can be readjusted by the options platform operator as and when there is a reason for such action.

In recent years, platform operators have introduced more short-term options for some underlying. Some are weekly, while others are on a fortnightly basis. These ones have the corresponding weekly or fortnightly expiries. When the life span of options run out, the operators then create new deadlines. However, all classes of options have their expiries subject to quarters of the financial calendar.

CHAPTER 2:

What Influences Options Prices?

Pricing is a complex subject when it comes to options trading. Not only is the price of an option based on the value of the asset, there are other external factors that have influence.

As an options trader, you want to make sure that you maximize your efforts to make a profit. Learning how to determine the prices you should pay for options is one of the basic ways that you can ensure that your yield is as high as it can be. You do not want to be stiffed by paying higher premiums than you should.

Pricing of options are determined by several factors. Each will be stated below.

The Value of the Asset

The effect this has on options prices is straightforward. If the value of this asset goes down, then exercising the option to sell becomes more valuable while the right to buy is become less valuable.

On the other hand, if the value increases, the right to sell it becomes less valuable while the right to buy it becomes more appealing due to this increase.

The Intrinsic Value

When an options trader pays a premium, this sum represents two values. The premium is made up of the intrinsic value, which is the current value of the option and the potential increase in value that this option can obtain over time. This potential increase over time is known as the time value.

We are discussing the intrinsic value. The intrinsic value is how much money the option is currently worth. It represents what the buyer would receive if he or she decided to exercise the option at the current time.

Intrinsic value is calculated by determining the difference in the current price of an asset and a strike price of the option. For an option to have an intrinsic value of zero, the option must be out of money. Therefore, the buyer would not exercise the option because this would result in a loss. The common strategy here is allowing the option to expire so that no pay off is made. As a result, the intrinsic value results in nothing to the buyer.

For a buyer to be in the money, the intrinsic value has to be greater than the premium to increase the value of the option. This place the buyer in a position to make a profit. The intrinsic value of for in the money for call options and put options are calculated slightly different. The formulas are as follows:

The Time Value

This value is the additional amount an investor is willing to contribute to the premium of an option in addition to the intrinsic value. This willingness stems from the belief that an option will increase in value before the expiration date reaches. Typically, an investor is only willing to put forth this extra amount if the option expires months away. There would be little to no change in the value of an option in a few days.

The time value is calculated by finding the difference between the intrinsic value of an option and the premium. The formula looks like this:

Option Premium - Intrinsic Value = Time Value

Therefore, the total price of an option premium follows this formula:

Intrinsic Value + Time Value = Option Premium

Both time value and intrinsic value help traders understand the value of what they are paying for if they decide to purchase an option. While the intrinsic value represents the worth of the option if the buyer were to exercise it at the current time, the time value represents the possible future value before or on the expiration date. These two values are important because they help traders understand the risk versus the reward of considering an option.

Volatility

This describes how likely a price change will occur during a specified amount of time on the financial market. If a financial market is nonvolatile then the prices change very slowly or remain totally unaffected over a specific amount of time. Volatile markets, on the other hand, have fast-changing prices over short periods of time.

Option traders can make use of a financial market's volatility to get a higher yield for their investment in the future. Options traders normally avoid slow-changing financial markets because these non-volatile markets often mean that no potential profit is available to the trader. Therefore, option traders thrive on volatility even though volatility increases the risk of option trading. As a result, an options trader needs to know how to read the financial market correctly to know which options are likely to yield the highest returns. This ability comes with experience, continuous learning and keeping up to date on the happenings of the financial markets.

There are many factors that affect the volatility of a financial market. These factors include politics, national economics and news reports. Options traders typically use one of two options strategies to gain the best yield from volatile markets. They are called straddle strategy and the strangle strategy.

Interest Rates

Most people are familiar with the term interest rates. Interest rates apply to mortgages bank accounts and more. Interest rates as it applies to option trading is slightly different from the common variations.

The interest rate is defined as the percentage of a particular rate for the use of money lent over a period of time. This interest rate of an option has different effects on the call option and put option. The premiums for call options rise when interest rates rise and fall when interest rates fall. The effect is the opposite on puts options. The premiums for put options fall when interest rates rise and rise when interest rates fall.

Interest rates affect the time value of options no matter what category they fall in!

You will come across the term risk-free interest rate many times in your study of options trading. This is described as the return made on an investment with no loss of capital. This is a misleading term because all investments carry some level of risk, no matter how minute. This more serves as a parameter in options pricing models such as the Black-Scholes Model to determine the premium that should be paid.

Dividends

Dividends are distributions of portions of a company's profit at a specified period. This distribution must be decided and managed by the board of directors of a company. It is paid to a particular class of shareholders. Dividends can be distributed in the form of cash, shares of stock and other types of property. Exchange-traded funds and mutual funds also pay out dividends.

As it relates to options trading, options do not actually pay dividends. However, the associated assets attached to that option can have them and thus, options trader can receive those dividends if he or she exercises that option and takes ownership of those particular assets. While both call and put options can be affected by the presence of dividends of the associated asset, this effect on the types of options is widely varied. While the presence of dividends makes call options less expensive due to the anticipation of a drop in price, it makes put options more expensive because the price will be decreased by the amount of the dividend.

Option Pricing Models

Option pricing theory uses all of the variables mentioned above to theoretically calculate the value of an option. It is a tool that allows trainers to get an estimate of an options fair value as they incorporate different strategies to maximize profitability. Luckily, there are models that traders can use to implement option pricing strategies to their advantage.

Three commonly used pricing models for option values are:

The Black-Scholes Model

Binomial Option Pricing Model

Monte-Carlo Simulations

The Black Scholes Model

Also known as the Black-Scholes-Merton (BSM) model, this pricing model won a Nobel Prize in economics because of its effectiveness. It was designed by the three economists, Fischer Black, Robert Merton and Myron Scholes in 1973. Originally used to price European options (meaning the option can only be exercised on the expiration date), this is a mathematical system that has a huge influence of modern option pricing. The pricing model helps differentiate options from gambling by determining the option premium to be paid in a logical manner. It calculates the return on the income the investor is likely to earn less the amount paid.

As this is primarily used to determine a European call option, the formula used to calculate it looks like this:

$SN(d1) - Xe - rt\ N(d2) = $ Call Option Premium

The letter representations in this equation stand for:

S – Current asset price

N – A normal distribution

X – Strike price

r – risk-free interest rate

t – time of maturity

While this pricing system is great, it does have limitations. One of these limitations is that it assumes that factors like volatility and risk-free interest will remain constant, which is not the case in actuality. It also does not factor in other costs to setting up the option.

Binomial Option Pricing Model

More commonly used to develop pricing for American options, this pricing system was developed in 1979. Even as popular as the Black Scholes Model is, this model is even more frequently used in practice because it is more intuitive. This pricing system allows for the assumption that there are two possible outcomes – one where the outcome moves up and one where the outcome moves down.

This system differs from the Black Scholes Model in the way that it allows calculations for multiple periods whereas the Black Scholes Model does not. This advantage gives a multi-period view, which is very advantageous to options traders.

This model makes use of binomial trees to figure out options pricing. These are diagrams with a main formula branching off into two different directions. This branching off is what gives the multi-period view that this pricing system is famous for.

For this pricing system to work, the following assumptions are made:

There are 2 possible prices for the associated asset, hence the name of the pricing system. Bi means 2.

The 2 possibilities involve the price of the asset moving up or down.

There are no dividends being paid on the asset.

The rate of interest does not change through the life of the option

There are no risks attached to the transaction.

There are no other costs associated with the option.

Clearly, just like with the Black Scholes Model, there is some limitation with those assumptions. Still, the pricing system is highly valuable in the valuing of American options due to the fact that such options can be exercise any time until the expiration date.

Monte Carlo Simulations

Used in multiple fields across the board like science, engineering and finance, this model allows the options trader to consider multiple outcomes due to the involvement of random factors. It allows for the consideration of risk and unpredictability unlike the first two pricing models. This is why it is also sometimes called multiple probability simulation.

A Final Word on Pricing

The reason I went into such depth on pricing options is because I want you to realize that everything related to options requires careful consideration right down to the premiums paid. This needs to be a fair trade for all the parties involved and premium pricing needs to reflect that fairness. When considering the options premium, remember to search deeper than the surface level to ensure that fairness and to ensure that you are gaining the profit that you need out of the transaction.

CHAPTER 3:

The Trader Mindset

Someone who is new to the idea of trading in options is only going to concern themselves with making money. They are going to celebrate big time when their traders are profitable, and then they will ignore the trades that lose money. This may be a natural thing for them, but it is a bad idea. The path to becoming a long-term and successful trader means that you need to not only pay attention when the trades are going your way, but you also need to understand why some of your trades lose money. When you do this, it becomes much easier to reduce the number of trades that are failing because you learn what to avoid overall.

No matter how long you are in the market, you will sometimes make winning trades in options, and other times you will make losing trades. As you spend more time options trading, you will get better at reading the market and using the strategies in the proper manner. But there will still be times when the trades won't go the way that you are.

Trading psychology is the mental state and emotions that determine the success or failure of trading options.

It represents the aspect of your behavior that dictates the decisions you make when faced with a trade. The psychology is vital to any trade and can be compared to experience, knowledge, and skills in determining your success as a trader.

When you decide to start options trading, you need to grasp the concept of risk-taking and discipline that determine the implementation of any trade.

The two most common emotions are greed and fear, while others are regret and hope.

We associate trading psychology to some behaviors and emotions that are often the triggers for catalysts for decisions. The most common emotions that every trader will come across is fear and greed.

Fear

At any given time, fear represents one of the worst kinds of emotions that you can have. Check in your newspaper one day, and you read about a steep selloff, and the next thing is trying to rack your brain about what to do next even if it isn't the right action at that time.

Many investors think that they know what will happen in the next few days, which makes them have a lot of confidence in the outcome of the trade. This leads to investors getting into the trade at a level that is too high or too low, which in turn makes them react emotionally.

As the trader puts a lot of hope on the single trade, the level of fear tends to increase, and hesitation and caution kick in.

Fear is part of every trader, but skilled traders have the capacity to manage the fear. There are various types of fears that you will experience, let us look at a few of them:

The Fear to Lose

Have you ever entered a trade and all you could think about is losing? The fear of losing makes it hard for you to execute the perfect strategy or enter or exit a strategy at the right time.

As a trader, you know that you need to make timely decisions when the strategy signals you to take one. When you be afraid guiding you, the level of confidence drops, and you don't have the ability to execute the strategy the right way, at the right time. When a strategy fails, you lose trust in your abilities as well as strategy.

When you lose trust in many of the strategies, you end up with analysis paralysis, whereby you don't have the capacity to pull the trigger on any decision that you make. Making a move becomes a huge challenge.

When you cannot pull the trigger, all you can think about is staying away from the pain of losing, while you need to move towards gains.

No trader likes to lose, but it is a fact that even the best traders will make losses once in a while. The key is for them to make more profitable trades that allow them to stay in the game.

When you worry too much, you end up being distracted from your execution process, and instead, you focus on the results.

To reduce the fear in trading, you need to accept losses. The probability of losing or making a profit is 50/50, and you need to accept this fact and accept a trade, whether it is a sell or a buy signal.

The Fear of a Positive Trend Going Negative (and Vice Versa)

Many traders choose to go for quick profits and then leave the losses to run down. Many traders want to convince themselves that they have made some money for the day, so they tend to go for a quick profit so that they have the winning feeling.

So, what should you do instead? You need to stick with the trend. When you notice a trend is starting, it is good to stay with the trend until you have a signal that the trend is about to reverse. It is only then that you exit this position.

To understand this concept, you need to consider the history of the market. History is good at pointing out that times change, and trends can go either way. Remember that no one knows the exact time the trend will start or end; all you need to do is wait upon the signal.

The Fear of Missing Out

For every trade, you have people that doubt the capacity of the trade to go through. After you place the trade, you will be faced with many skeptics that will doubt the whole procedure and leave you wondering whether to exit the strategy or not.

This fear is also characterized by greed – because you aren't working on the premise of making a successful trade rather the fact that the security is rising without you having a piece of the pie.

This fear is usually based on information that there is a trend which you missed that you would have capitalized on.

This fear has a downside – you will forget about any potential risk associated with the trade and instead think that you have the capacity to make a profit because other people benefited from the action.

Fear of Being Wrong

Many traders put too much emphasis on being right that they forget that this is a business they should run the right way. They also forget that being successful is all about knowing the trend and how it affects their engagement.

When you follow the best timing strategy, you create many positive results over a certain time.

The uncanny desire to focus on always being right instead of focusing on making money is a great part of your ego, and to stay on the right path; you need to trade without your ego for once.

31

If you accommodate a perfectionist mentality when you get into trades, you will be after failure because you will experience a lot of losses as well. Perfectionists don't take losses the right way, and this translates into fear.

Ways to Overcome Fear in Trading

As you can see, it is obvious that fear can lead to losses. So, how can you avoid this fear and become successful?

Learn

You need to find a way to get knowledge so that you have the basis for making decisions. When you know all there is to know about options, you know what to buy and when to sell, and learn which ones to watch. You are then more comfortable making the right decisions.

Envision the bigger picture

You always need to evaluate your choices at all times and see what you have gained or lost so far for taking some steps. Understanding the mistakes, you made gives you guidance to make better decisions in the future.

Start Small

Many traders that subscribe to fear have lost a lot before. They put a lot of funds on the line and ended up losing, which in turn made them fear to place other trades. Begin with small sums so that you don't risk too much to put fear in you. Once you get more confident, you can invest larger sums so that you enjoy more profit.

Use the Right Strategy

Having the right trading strategy makes it easy to execute your trades successfully. Make sure you look at various options trading strategies so that you know which one is ideal for your situation and skills.

Many strategies can help you succeed, but others might leave you confused. If you have a strategy that doesn't give you the returns you desire, then adjust it to suit your needs over time. Refine it till you are comfortable with its performance.

Go Simple

When you have a strategy that is simple and straightforward, you will be less likely to lose confidence along the way because you know what to expect.

Additionally, the easier the strategy, the faster it will be to spot any issues.

Don't Hesitate

At times you have to jump into the fray even if you aren't so comfortable with the way it works. Once you begin taking steps, you will learn more about the trade.

However, you need always to be prepared when taking any trade. The more prepared you are, the easier it will be for you to run successful trades.

Don't Give Up

Things might not always go as you expect them to do. Remember that mistakes are there to give you lessons that will make you a better trader. When you lose, take time to identify the mistake you made and then correct it, then try again.

Greed

This refers to a selfish desire to get more money than you need from a trade. When the desire to get more than you can usually make takes over your decision-making process, you are looking at failure.

Greed is seen to be more detrimental than fear. Yes, fear can make you lose trades, but the good thing is that you get to preserve your capital. On the other hand, greed places you in a situation where you spend your capital faster than you return it. It pushes you to act when you shouldn't be acting at all.

The Danger of Being Greedy

When you are greedy, you end up acting irrationally. Irrational trading behavior can be overtrading, overleveraging, holding onto trades for too long, or chasing different markets.

The more greed you have, the more foolish you act. If you reach a point at which greed takes over from common sense, then you are overdoing it.

When you are greedy, you also end up risking way much more than you can handle, and you end up with a loss. You also have unrealistic expectations from the market, which makes it seem as if you are after just money and nothing else.

When you are greedy, you also start trading prematurely without any knowledge of the options trading market.

When you are too greedy, your judgment is clouded, and you won't think about any negative consequences that might result when you make certain decisions.

Many traders that were too greedy ended up giving up after making this mistake in the initial trading phase.

How to Overcome Greed

Like any other endeavors in trading, you need a lot of efforts to overcome greed. It might not be easy because we are talking about human emotions here, but it is possible.

First, you have to know that every call you make won't be the right one at all times. There are times when you won't make the right move, and you will end up losing money. At times you will miss the perfect strategy altogether, and you won't move a step ahead.

Secondly, you have to agree that the market is way bigger than you. When you do this, you will accept and make mistakes in the process.

CHAPTER 4:

Basic Trading with Covered Calls

What is Buying a Covered Call

Buying a covered call means that you're buying a stock at a certain price. For example, let's say that you are looking to buy some IBM stock. Instead of writing to get it at a certain price, you are buying it from the trader at a certain price, when the stock falls below a certain level.

So, let's say the IBM stock is trading at $45 currently. You buy a covered call that says the stock will be sold at $40 a share. So, the stock goes up to $47, and you get that stock for $40, and essentially, you're saving $700 on the stock price. If it goes down to $39 somehow, you can't exercise this, and then, you end up losing out on the premium, whatever that may be.

Selling Covered Calls

As a beginner, most people choose to dip their toes in the complicated waters of options trading through selling covered calls. It's arguably the most basic level of options trading and, while also not the most adrenaline-inducing, a great way to find your feet before moving on to more complicated strategies.

Selling covered calls is also likely to be an aspect of your options portfolio in the long term. Many traders use it as a steady way of generating income – a conservative baseline for their account.

A third benefit to starting with covered calls is that it includes the majority of the knowledge and strategy that you will use as an options trader, so it's a perfect training ground.

Using this strategy, you are going to be selling the right to buy underlying stocks that you own. A "covered" call is so called because you own those shares, therefore you have the sale covered.

Before you can begin, therefore, you will need to own at least 100 shares, or one stock. By writing an option for those shares, you are offering buyers the right to buy them by the expiration date if the share price hits your strike price.

When a buyer takes advantage of your offer, you will receive the premium. That's yours to take home – you will never have to give it back, whether the strike price is met, and the buyer exercises their right or not. That, right there, is your reason for selling covered calls: the steady influx of cash from the premiums.

It's also a good way to sell your stock – a clever trader will use this type of strategy to clear their portfolio of shares they no longer want to own. There are advantages to owning that stock in the interim, too. If it goes up in price, you may receive dividends and you'll receive capital gains (the difference between the price now and the increased price at time of sale) when the deadline arrives.

Strategy for Selling Covered Calls

We've covered the process, but what about the strategy behind it? We looked at the absolute basics of that strategy, but an experienced trader knows there's always going to be more to an option than meets the eye.

There's a whole list of considerations that you will eventually want to bear in mind as you expand your knowledge and develop your own, personal strategy. Every trader has a different attitude towards what works and what doesn't – there are plenty of ways to make selling a covered call work, but you'll probably find yourself preferring one or two strategies.

We'll take a look now at those considerations in more detail to guide you as you delve into the covered call more deeply:

The Market Environment: You are no doubt aware that traders of stocks and shares are happy in a bull market and disgruntled in a bear market. You may also know that such traders hate a flat market most of all, because very little is happening and there aren't many big profits to be made. For you, as a seller of covered calls, the opposite is true. I highly recommend waiting for the market to temporarily flatten before embarking on a spate of covered call sales. This is because you're only really interested in small changes to your share prices – if they are skyrocketing, you're losing more money on your contract. There also isn't as much danger of the bottom falling out of the market and your stock prices plummeting at the same time, which would be problematic.

Your Underlying Stock: There is nothing more important to your success than choosing the right stocks to invest in in the first place. I cannot stress strongly enough that your success will be heightened if you pick stocks that move up very slowly. You don't want stocks that rise and fall very quickly, especially as a beginner, because they have a habit of making surprising moves that ruin your strategy. If they drop too far, you stand to lose a lot of money in the sale; if they rise too high, you lose the money you could have made if you'd sold them at that price.

The Premium: Always remember that the premium is your guaranteed profit. Whatever else happens, you're going to walk away with that cash. When you factor in the cost to list the option and any commission you will lose to your broker, you'll be able to calculate the actual profit you'll make on that premium. Set yourself a minimum premium – a number that you consider to be enough to provide a profit you'll be happy with, on the assumption that it's the only profit you make. When you move ahead on setting the strike price, you'll likely adjust this base figure up or down based on what you think the underlying stock is going to do before the expiration date.

The Expiration Date: There's a reason that the premiums on covered calls get higher the further out the expiration date. It's because, much like the weather forecasts we all deride on a daily basis, it gets harder and harder to predict what's going to happen to a share price the further out you go. Also bear in mind that your money is going to be tied up until the expiration date, so the premium will increase as a nod to that sacrifice. Most investors believe that a time span of between a month and three months works best.

The Strike Price: You might think that the strike price you set should be based on what you, as the seller, are comfortable with, but actually it's the opposite. You're looking for a strike price that your buyer will feel comfortable with, because otherwise they aren't going to buy. That, in turn, is going to be dictated by the expiration date you set, as well as the premium you're asking for and how stable or volatile the underlying stock is.

With all these factors in mind, you are likely starting to see that there is no single "correct decision" when it comes to selling covered calls. It's going to take practice and concentration to figure out which ones work best for you.

It's also important to note that your strategy is probably going to change as you gain experience. The more options you sell, the more you will see new and more advanced ways to take advantage of the market. For now, I urge you to be conservative in your approach and accept that selling covered options is not going to win you your fortune – but it is going to help you increase the seed money you have available to do just that.

Finding the Right Stock and Strike Price for a Covered Call

So how do you find the right stock for this? Well, again you want to find a stock that is going to have enough volatility where it will get to the price that you want it to be, pays decent dividends, and also is a field that will actually be around for a while.

One that currently is thriving is DSL actually. You may think that it isn't going to do as well, but it still holds an impressive number of dividends. That means if you can find stocks that are being sold, that have the potential to possibly change the game for the better later on, and also are worth investing in, you should do that.

You should look for a stock that you have a feeling you can easily get too. If there are a lot of open interests on the stock, I do suggest possibly taking your time and putting effort into that. You'd be amazed at the difference it can make.

How to Buy a Successful Covered Call

So, let's talk about how you buy a covered call and a stock that you want to have. How do you do it? Well, the answer is simple.

First, you must take a look at the stock that you want to buy, the shares, and what you're going to need to pay, especially against those premiums.

So, let's say you want to buy stock with Ford, because hey, Ford is releasing a new engine and car set, and you have a feeling it will increase in price. You can do this with Apple as well because there are rumors the MacBook Pro 2019 is coming out next month or something. Lots of people like to jump on the apple covered calls right before the reveals of their iPhones. So, you log into your account, and from there look for the stock that has a price in the range that you want. You want the strike price to be a decent amount, such as maybe 14 dollars a share per 100 shares. Now, when you're inside, you choose the call that you want to buy, and maybe you choose that call option and look to see how many days this will go. You should from there, choose the option to get this call. Once you're going to do there, if you're going to right click, and choose what you want to do with the covered stock and choose that you want a contract for this one. You may be taken at this point to the page to fill out the information, and you should from there, look to see what your cost basis is going to be, and the amount that you're going to pay. You should look for a decent price on the shares, and make sure that you're not letting them fall too much.

If the stock is falling, do not take it. That's a sinking ship, and you can say goodbye to that. But, once you choose this, you then will start to look at the stock, and once you see that the shares are at a higher price than what you bought the covered call for, you can then log in, and choose to exercise this.

At this point, once you've exercised it, the investor will be obligated to sell you the option, and from there, you can now buy the covered call option that you want at the price that is listed.

Now, let's take the flip side. Suppose maybe you didn't see the trends changing all that much, and it became a stagnated stock. Unfortunately, the longer you hold out, the less fluctuation is going to happen on the stock. Your goal is to get out of there as fast as possible. The problem is, over time, that stock will stay at that range. You want to invest the moment you know there is a big change.

So yes, right before the Apple reveal will be great, the stock goes up, you cash in on that option immediately. But, let's say that it's been a slower month, and you end up not doing anything with it. Well, the investor you bought it from will get to collect it.

CHAPTER 5:

In The Money, Out of The Money

In the Money

Before we get to that, let's review some important market jargon. The first term we need to know is called "in the money." Calls are easier for people to understand because if you are not experienced as an in-depth market trader you are not used to thinking in terms of shorting stocks. Normal people want stock prices to rise. As you learn more about options trading, you will find out that it is not always the best thing. But calls have an intrinsic appeal to that natural belief, thought process, and desire.

A call option *is* called in the money when the price in the market of a certain stock is above than the average strike price of the option. So, if you have an option with a strike price of $75 and the stock is trading at $80 a share, it is in the money. In short, in the money call options are worth a lot more than options that are not in the money. We can take a look at the options calculator to see what the differences can be.

So, I have set up a hypothetical stock which is trading at $80 dollars a share. We will consider an option that expires in 14 days. Just for the record, the implied volatility is 16%, and the risk-free rate is 0.3% (we will explain what that means in a minute).

Setting the strike price at $75 we find that the option (in this case a call) is priced at $5.03. Once again remember that is for a single share, the total price of the option would be $503.

Now let's consider another option with all the same characteristics but say that this one has a strike price of $70. The price of this option is $10.01, or $1001 to buy the option. The option with the strike price of $70 is also in the money, but it's more in the money then the option with the strike price of $75. Another way to express this concept is by saying that it is deeper in the money.

If the share price is exactly equal to the strike price, the option is said to be at the money. The odds of an option being exactly at the money in the real world are slim, but they can be very close to at the money. These types of options can be of interest because, if the stock price goes beyond the strike, the value of the option can suddenly increase by a large margin.

For a call option, the probability of the share price moving above the strike price can actually be fairly high. Using the example of a strike price at $75, the price of the option would be $0.92 (you would have to pay $92 to purchase the option). If the share price rises to $76 later that afternoon, the price of that call will jump to $1.53.

This kind of price change illustrates why people find trading options so appealing. If you sold right then, that would net you $61 in profit for each options contract.

Out of the Money

When the strike price is higher than the share price on the market, we say that the option is out of the money.

Options don't need to be in the money in order to make a profit. Depending on the direction of price movement, you can earn profits from out of the money options as well. We can illustrate this with call options.

If the stock price is rising, the prices of out of the money calls are going to rise as well. So, we shall set up a similar scenario where there are 14 days until option expiration, but, this time, assume that the strike price is $77. Suppose the share price is $75 which is lower than the strike, the option is out of the money.

If the share price rises over the next couple of days, you can actually make a decent profit. The good thing about out of the money options is they are relatively cheap.

Using our example, the $77 strike would cost $0.27 ($27 to buy).

Now let's suppose that, two days later, the share price rises to $76.50. The option is still out of the money. However, the price of the option will rise because the share price is rising. It turns out that under these conditions the price of the option would be $0.66 at that point. That means you could turn around and sell it for $66 when you had purchased it two days earlier for $27.

Many experts don't recommend trading out of the money options. But they remain a great alternative for people that don't have much money to start making profits. This can work if there is a large price move for the underlying stock and you only hold the option for a couple of days. If there is a lot of movement within a single day, you can actually make substantial profits.

Let's consider a real option for Apple. Consider one with the strike price of $220 that expires in 16 days. At market opening, Apple was $192.50 a share. At that time the call option was priced at $0.08: you could have purchased each options contract for a mere $8. Later in the morning, the share price of Apple rose to $195.76. That drove the price of the $200 strike price option to $0.16 (or for all 100 shares, $16). So, we would have an opportunity to double our money, and to make it significant you could buy multiple options simultaneously. Remember to always check the liquidity. Looking at the volume, it is 102 for that option and the open interest is 269. That would be enough liquidity to close the position in a timely fashion.

One thing to remember about options is that If an option expires and it is out of the money, it is also worthless (it "expires worthless"). This holds true for at the money options as well. If the option is in the money at expiration, the price of the option is (share price – the strike price).

CHAPTER 6:

Stepping Up in Trading with Calls

A call choice contract gives the holder the privilege to buy 100 offers of the stock (per contract) at the fixed strike value, which does not change, paying little mind to the real market cost of the capital. A case of a call alternative contract would be:

1 PKT Dec 40 Call with a premium of $500. PKT is the stock you are buying the agreement on. One implies One alternative contract speaking to 100 offers of PKT. The fundamental idea and figuring out how to trade call options in this model is you are paying $500, which is 100% in danger if you don't do anything with the agreement before December, yet you reserve the privilege to buy 100 offers of the stock at 40. Thus, if PKT shoots up to 60. You can practice the agreement and buy 100 offers of it at 40. When you quickly sell the stock in the open market, you would understand a benefit of 20 points or $2000. You paid a premium of $500 so the total net increase in this options trading model would be $1500. So, the main concern is, you generally need the market to rise when you are long or have obtained a call choice.

Trading Strategy versus Practicing and Understanding Premiums

With call options, the exceptional will ascend as the market on the first stock ascents. Buyer request will increment. This expansion in premiums considers the financial specialist to trade the choice in the market for a benefit. So, you are not practicing the agreement, however, repurchasing it. The distinction in the superior you paid and the excellent it was sold for, will be your benefit. The advantage for individuals hoping to figure out how to trade options or get familiar with the nuts and bolts of a trading strategy is you don't have to buy a stock through and through to benefit from its expansion with calls.

Why Invest in Call Options?

You buy a call option when you are bullish on a stock. In other words, you buy a call option when you are expecting the price of the underlying stock to rise. Theoretically, if you are buying a call option, you are hoping to buy shares of stock at the strike price, which you expect to be lower than the market price at some point.

So, let's say that a stock is trading at $99 a share. You could buy a call option with a strike price of $100 a share, if there is a consensus that the stock is going to see a significant rise in prices before the option expires. Say for the sake of example that the option costs you $1. Options prices are quoted on a per share basis, so that means you have to spend $100 to buy the option.

Now say that before the option expires, the share price goes up as expected, say to $103 a share. Now you have two possibilities. When the price of the underlying stock goes up, the value of the option contract goes up as well. Maybe the price of the option has risen to $1.50 per share, say. So, in that case, you can simply sell the option and take the $0.50 per share profit.

You can also choose to exercise the option. This means you can buy the stock at the strike price of $100 a share, even though the market price of the stock has risen to $103 a share. So, your total expense is now $101 a share since you paid $1 to buy the option (assuming zero commissions, which is reasonable these days). So now, you can turn around and sell the stock at $103 a share on the open market, earning yourself a profit of $2 a share. And in some cases, investors may decide to keep the stock that they have now been able to purchase at a discount.

Breakeven Price

An important concept in options trading is the breakeven price. For a call option, the breakeven price is the strike price + the price paid to buy the option, on a per share basis. So, if you are buying an option with a strike price of $212 for $2.50, the breakeven price is simply $212 + $2.50 = $214.50. This means that the share price must rise to at least $214.50 before exercising the option even warrants consideration, otherwise you would be losing money as a buyer. For options sellers, the breakeven price is important to note as well. If you are selling to open call options, you don't have to worry if the market price of the stock stays at or below the breakeven price. In this example, a call options seller would be fine as long as the stock price stayed at or below $214.50.

The Call Seller

An options contract goes on the market when a seller "writes" the contract. For retail traders (individual, small traders) you sell to open from a list of available options. So, you would find a call option with an expiration date and strike price that you like, and then you sell it using your brokerage software. There are three ways that you can sell a call option, the most basic way is to sell a covered call. To do this, you would need 100 shares of the underlying stock. Keep in mind that there is a risk you will lose ownership of the shares; in the event the option is exercised, and the shares are "called away" from you. But a carefully selected strike price and expiration date can lower your risk. The goal of selling a covered call option is to generate income from shares of stock that you own. Remember that the breakeven price is going to be something to keep your eye on in this case.

Another way that call options are sold is as a part of one of the options strategies that we will be looking at later, such as an iron condor or a debit spread. In those types of strategies, there is a single transaction involving multiple options that are bought and sold, and so using a strategy you are never going to be selling a single option.

Finally, you can sell a call option "naked", which means that you don't own the shares of stock. You must be a level four trader in order to sell naked options.

The call seller has a risk of assignment. That means, if the share price rises above the breakeven price, a buyer of an option may choose to exercise the option. As a seller you will be assigned and that means you will be forced to sell 100 shares of stock at the strike price. Many articles about options will assert that most options expire worthless, but the reality is if the option you have sold goes "in the money", there is a real risk that the option will be exercised. In fact, options that expire in the money are often automatically exercised by the broker. Check with your broker to find out their specific policies.

Profits from Call Options

If you are buying call options, then you are hoping to make a profit from either exercising the option or simply selling it at a profit. Most beginning options traders are going to be working with smaller amounts of capital, and so you are probably not going to be interested in exercising the option. Rather, you are going to earn profits from the option itself. As the price of the underlying stock increases, the value of a call option increases as well.

There are several factors working in options pricing, and so you have to take more than just the underlying price of the stock into account. The most important of these is the expiration date. Simply put, the more time there is until an option expires, the more valuable it is. The value in the options price is referred to as time value, and it also makes up a part of "extrinsic" value of the option. With each passing day, the option will lose time value. As we will see next, you can actually look up the amount of value that an option is going to lose the following day. At market open, that amount is automatically deducted from the options price. That doesn't mean you can't hold options overnight, because other factors will be operating to push up the price of the option as well, and this may overwhelm the decline in price from the loss of time value. This loss of time value is called "time decay".

Options that are out of the money are the most susceptible to time decay, and if they are out of the money as the expiration date approaches, they can be worth hardly anything. When the option actually expires, they are not worth any money at all. That is why we say they "expire worthless".

The most important factor in the price of the option, therefore, is the underlying share price on the open market. For a call option, whenever the share price increases, the value of the option is going to increase. This happens most strongly for in the money options, but all call options will increase in value when there is a movement upward in the share price. So, you can even earn significant profits from out of the money options on a day when there are large upward movements in the price of the stock. These movements don't have to be particularly large; a single dollar rise in share price can mean anywhere from a $50 to $100 increase in the price of an option. So, you could buy an option in the morning and if the share price rises by a dollar during the day, you could sell it for a $50 to $100 profit. The more the share price rises, the more profit is possible. While out of the money options will often yield lower profit amounts for a given share price movement, the profits can still be substantial.

So, for basic options trading, the idea behind buying a call option is simple. You hope to buy low and sell high, earning profits from the upward price movement of the underlying stock. Your goal is to sell the option before expiration and before time decay eats up some or all of the gains (in the case of out of the money options).

CHAPTER 7:

Buying and Selling Puts

Put Option

If you expect the price of a stock to drop, you can profit from this by investing in put options. Put options work in many ways in the same manner as call options. They have an expiration date, they have 100 shares of underlying stock, and their price depends on the price of the underlying stock. Meanwhile, they also suffer from time decay as the expiration date of the option approaches. However, put options actually gain value when the stock price drops, and they lose value when the stock price rises.

This means that put options can be used to "short" the stock. Shorting the stock is just jargon for earning a profit when the stock price declines. Normally, shorting a stock works like this. If you think that a stock is going to drop in value, you borrow shares from your broker – and you immediately sell them on the market at the current stock price. Then, assuming that your bet was the correct one, you buy the shares back when the price drops. Suppose for the sake of example that when you initially borrowed the shares, you sold them at $100 a share. Then the price drops to $80 a share –

maybe the company had a bad earnings call, for example. When the price drops, you buy the shares back at $80 a share, and you return them to the broker (remember, you started the process by borrowing shares from the broker). This exercise leaves you with a $20 per share profit.

Of course, most small investors don't have $10,000 or more to chance on schemes like this, but put options enable you to earn profits if the price of a stock declines, using much smaller investments. The idea is basically the same, but when you suspect that the price of a stock is going to drop in the near future, you can buy put options on the stock. A put option has a strike price just like a call option, and when the share price is below the strike price, the put option is in the money. That's because you would be able to buy shares of stock at the market price, and then sell them at the strike price – earning a profit in the process.

Using the same example, we considered before, you could buy a put option with a $100 strike price. Then when the price of the shares dropped to $80, you could buy them on the market, and then sell them to the originator of the put option contract at the strike price - $100 a share. Buying a put option is something that doesn't require a large margin account to do.

When a put option is exercised, that is you sell the stock at the strike price, they say that the stock was "put to" the originator of the option contract. Of course, most options traders are not looking to exercise individual put options. If the stock price were really to drop $20 a share on a stock where you bought put options with a $100 strike price, the value of the put options would go up substantially, because you could exercise them and make solid profits. Since there are other traders who would be interested in selling the stock, you will be able to sell your put option to another trader for a profit. Remember that if you buy to open an options contract, you are not obligated to anything and are free and clear once you sell it to someone else.

Think of put options in the same way as call options, but with the price going up $100 every time the stock drops by $1. Like call options, the pricing of put options is impacted by many factors, and so this is an ideal relationship that we are thinking about here. But it gives you a rule of thumb to understand how put options work (the more in the money they are, the closer they are going to get to the ideal case). Likewise, if the price of the stock rises by $1, the value of a put option would move down by $100. So, with put options, it's an inverse relationship.

Why Buy Put Options

You buy put options when you believe the value of a stock is going to decline. If a company has a bad earnings call, this can be a good time to buy a put option. Typically, the price of the stock will drop a lot, possibly over a day or two, and then stabilize at a new, lower level. Any bad news of any kind provides an opportunity to profit from put options. This is a kind of flexibility that doesn't exist for most stock traders and investors, being able to earn money when stocks are declining. The fact that you can open your eyes to the potential that options have in expanding your ability to make profits from the stock market. An options trader has the ability to profit under all possible scenarios of stock market movements.

CHAPTER 8:

Strategies for New Traders:
Long vs Short

Short Term Strategy

The use of a short-term strategy is intended to make as much money as possible in the short run, meaning on a day to day basis, or in periods of about a week. On the whole, "short term" refers to anything that's less than a month. Of course, there are some investors who plan their moves on an hourly basis. So, the concept of "short-term" does have varying degrees. It should be noted that short-term strategies are quite popular with novice investors as they are able to reduce the likelihood of risk by entering and exiting trades before any serious market fluctuations take place. As investors gain more experience, they can get a better feel for the way markets behave thus allowing them to stay in the game longer.

20-Day System

This is one of the techniques we use to make some short-term gains. If you look at the stock that has recently gone up, chances are it will go down drastically within 20 days. 99% of the time, this is the case, which is why we like to wait 20 days before we make any investment on a stock. If you wait 20 days, you will hit the lowest price point of that particular stock. When it is at its lowest, it is ideal that you invest your money into that stock. Chances are the stock will go up again, many top traders have been using this technique with fantastic success. The trick is to wait 20 days at least before you make a trade. Depending on the company, the stock prices will drop down within 20 days of it going up drastically. And on the 20th day, this is when you invest your money into that stock and see it grow. You can see capital gains within ten days of the spending that money.

To execute this strategy, it's a great idea to become very familiar with the 10-day moving average of the particular stock or asset you are looking to invest in. The 20-day strategy is two 10-day moving average periods. By observing this measure, you can determine where the trend of the stock lies. In this manner, you can estimate for the where prices may rise or fall. Although, an important thing to keep in mind is that you shouldn't account for trades lasting longer than a week. The reason for this is that 5 days is exactly half of the 10-day moving average. As such, you can come in and out well before markets recalibrate at the end of the week and then at the start of the week. It's always a good idea to get in the start of the week and be gone by Friday afternoon.

Don't Sell Until the Stock Price Hits Back up to Its All-Time High

After understanding the basics of the 20-day strategy, you need to know that you should not sell your stock unless and until it has gone back up to its highest stock price in those 20 days. Most of the time, when the stock hits its all-time low, it will rise again up to its all-time high if not higher, which is why it is advised that you wait for the stock to grow back up to its highest point or above. Meaning that you should not sell your stock unless and until it is leveled back up to its highest price point. A great rule of thumb would be to wait another 20 days after you've invested your money. Once you do that, except for the stock to climb back up, once it climbs back up to a price where it was at the highest or even higher than that, then you can most definitely pull out that money and enjoy it. We understand that you are always very emotional with the money you're investing.

A great piece of advice for novice investors is to avoid becoming emotionally attached to a stock or a particular deal. This is why options can help you take out the emotional component from trading. The reason for this lies in the fact investors feel that if they hold on just a little bit longer, then can offset their losses and recoup some profit. This is a flawed strategy. As such, it's always a good idea to cut your losses and move on when you can.

Look at the Trend

They must start looking at the pattern when you are trying to achieve short-term capital. Always look at the trends that are taking place and invest your money accordingly. If you have a feeling that a particular stock will go up in a short period, then make sure that you invest in that stock. If you look at the transcript history, then it shouldn't be hard for you to see which stocks will go up soon and which won't. This will allow you to make fantastic capital gains with your options trading. However, when following trends, you must keep an eye on your stock. As trends go, they will go up quickly, and they will go down even quicker. This is why it is ideal they keep checking up on your stock as much as possible and pull the trigger when you think it's right. As always do not get emotionally attached to your stocks and if you feel like it is slowly dropping down then perhaps sell the stock.

Control Risk

Risk is an inherent factor when it comes to trading. Consequently, it is imperative for you to manage risk in such a manner that you can cover yourself if, and when, markets suddenly turn. While this isn't all that frequent, there is always the possibility of a sudden event which can cause investors to sell off right away. In addition to purchasing options as a means of hedging your investments, never put in more than 2% of your investment capital into a single trade. What this does is that it spreads out the risk among the various deals you have going on at any one time. So, if one deal goes sour, the most you could potentially lose on that deal is 2%. On the contrary, if you invested, say, 50% of your capital on one deal, and that deal went sour, you'd lose half your investment capital. Needless to say, that would devastate your portfolio.

Target Stocks Which Will Make Big Moves Very Soon

Similar to looking at Trends, this is one of the long terms / short-term strategy options. The strategy can be both used in a long-term and short time. However, it's right to a short-term options trade, and you'll need to focus on stocks that have a history of making significant moves in a short period.

Long Term Strategy

We will talk about technical analysis and explain to you what it is and the same thing with the fundamental analysis. And then we will help you understand which method works better for what, once you've been able to understand this you will be in a much better position in terms of making more money with options trading.

Technical Analysis

To put with technical analysis, it is a way Option Traders finds a framework to study the price movement. The simple theory behind this method is that a person will look at the previous prices and the changes, hence determine the current trading conditions and the potential price movement. The only problem with this method would be that it is philosophical meaning that all technical analysis is that it is reflected in the price. The price reflects the information, which is out there, and the price action is all you would need to make a trade. The technical analysis banks on history and the trends, and the Traders will keep an eye on the past, and they will keep an eye on the future as well and based on that they will decide if they want to trade or not. More importantly, the people who are going to be trading using the technical analysis will use history to determine whether they're going to make the trade or not. Essentially the way to check out technical analysis would be to look up the trading price of a particular stock in five years. This is what many Option Traders used to determine the history and the future of the capital, and whether or not they should trade using technical analysis. There are many charts you can look up online to figure out how technical analysis takes place. However, we have given you a brief explanation of what technical analysis is.

Fundamental Analysis

Fundamental analysis is more realistic and feasible in the long term. The whole premise behind the theoretical analysis is that you look at the economy of the country and the trading system that's going on to determine whether it is a good trade or not. More focusing on economics, that's why it helps you to figure out which dollar is going up or down and what is causing it.

One of the greatest things you can do when it comes to Options Trading is to understand why a dollar is dropping or going up. Once you're able to understand that, you will be in a much better position for gaining profits in your Option Trading endeavors. When using the fundamental analysis, you will be looking at the country's employment and unemployment rate also see how the training with different countries overall sing the country's economy before you decide on whether you should try it or not. Many successful Option Traders solely believe in fundamental analysis, as it is factual, unlike technical analysis. Even though technical analysis is accurate, it is not guaranteed like the theoretical analysis. Instead of looking at the trends, you will be looking at what is causing the highs and the lows. Not only that, based on the highs and lows, you will be able to determine the country's current and future economic outlook, whether it is good or not. One rule of thumb to look into with be how good the state is doing, the better the state is doing, the more foreign investors are going to take part in it. Once starting the piece in it, the dollar or the stock in that country will go up tremendously.

The idea behind fundamental analysis is that you need to look at the country's economical, and you also need to look at it. To make you understand, what fundamental analysis is it is mostly when you invest in a country is doing good in the economy, and not invest in a company when they're doing wrong in the marketplace. Which makes sense since the economy dictates how high are low prices going to be per dollar? Most of the time, investors will invest the money as soon as they see the dollar going up. The reason why they will do that is that they know the dollar will keep climbing up since the economy is getting better. One of the great examples would be when the US dollar dropped in 2007 2008, and the Canadian dollar took up, at that point, a lot of investors are investing in Canadian dollars of the US dollar.

After a very long time, the US dollar was dropping tremendously, whereas the Canadian dollar was more expensive than the US dollar. This was one of the anomalies which took place back in the day.

CHAPTER 9:

Horizontal Spreads

Horizontal spreads, like their vertical cousins, are two legged trades. They're easy to setup but can be a bit tricky to analyze prior to entry. This is because most horizontal spreads have a time factor that makes them confuse to some people. All in all, the horizontal spread strategy is one which relies on a little bit of luck.

However, the times you do get it right makes it all worthwhile since the rewards tend to be higher when done well.

Call Calendar Spread

Horizontal spread trades are also called calendar spreads due to the way the two legs of the trade are setup. The call calendar spread is best used after the initial part of an uptrend when the trend begins to slow down. The best part of the calendar spread is that you can set pretty much any time frame you want the trade to work out in.

The first leg to establish is a long call position which has an expiry date at least 60 days out from the trade date. The second leg is a short call position which has an expiration of at least 30 days. The key thing to note is that the long call should expire after the short call does. The strike prices of both calls are the same.

You can see where the term horizontal or calendar comes from. Vertical spreads had you placing trades on calls and puts in the same expiration month but at different strike prices. Here, we're looking at the same strike price but with different expiration dates. This pushes the trade out horizontally.

You can choose an expiration for the long call to be greater than 60 days or even 90 days away. Similarly, you can shorten the time frame for the short call as well but remember that if you move within the 30-day period, time decay means you'll receive less of a premium upon writing the option.

Should you lengthen the time frame of the short call? You an but this is a risky thing to do as you'll see now.

Trade Premise

The idea behind a horizontal call spread is to essentially have you cake and eat it too. Uptrends can sometimes be sluggish. They can be long and drawn out and they can move sideways for long periods of time without losing any strength. This kind of behavior makes a short-term vertical spread unprofitable.

Imagine initiating a bull call spread knowing that price is going to move upwards for a long time but as time goes by, price simply sits there. All the while, your vertical spread trade doesn't do anything, and you end up paying money to enter the trade. You could initiate a bull put spread, but this seems like the wrong thing to do.

What I mean is that if you know that the trend is going to last for a long time, why would you limit your profit right upon entry? It doesn't make sense. This is where a horizontal trade makes far more sense since you can take advantage of both the short-term sluggishness as well as the long-term potential.

In technical terms, you will see such an opportunity in a trend where counter trend presence has grown, and ranges are lasting for a few weeks at a time. In such conditions, the short call (which has a closer expiry date) will help you capture the premium since price is unlikely to hit it. Once price breaks out of the range and moves upwards, the long call will move into the money and you'll be able to capture the profit from the bull move. Determining the correct strike price when it comes to horizontal trades is even more important than in vertical spreads. Thankfully, it isn't as difficult as it sounds. You need to look at the upcoming resistance levels and choose a price beyond it. Take care to not choose a level that is far too strong. Ideally, you want a level that is medium in strength and is going to hold for at least a month or so. Using TSLA as an example (market price $478.15,) let's assume $500 to be our ideal strike price. The 500-call expiring a month later will cost us $28.50. The 500-call expiring in 31 days will net us a premium of $20, making this a net debit trade to the tune of $8.50. The ideal scenario would be if TSLA were to stay below 500 for a month or so and then rise past it which will ensure both legs behave appropriately.

If the trade doesn't quite go how you want, you can adjust it to another strategy. Let's say TSLA looks like it will burst past 500 in the current month. At this point, you can adjust the trade to a bull call spread. You can cover your short call position and open another one expiring in the same month as the long call.

Similarly, if TSLA declines sharply and looks like it won't move past 500 anytime soon, you can adjust the trade to be a bear call spread. It depends on how you read the existing market conditions.

Put Spreads

Much like how you can take advantage of call spreads, you can do the same with put spreads. Again, none of the following strategies call for underlying stock ownership and thus, the risk, as well as the margin required to establish a position, is greatly reduced.

A number of these spread trades can be converted into a collar under suitable situations. As we move forward, keep this in mind since it isn't always possible to list out every single exit scenario. Keep in mind the conditions required for a successful collar trade and after reviewing the strategies, try to see how you could turn them into profitable collars.

As always, these strategies will make you money in bullish, bearish, and neutral market environments.

CHAPTER 10:

Straddles and Strangles

To round off our look at options trading strategies we're going to take a look at straddles and strangles. These are often referred to as combination trades. The reason for this is that they involve initiating legs which involve both calls and puts. These trades are another step up in terms of complexity but once again, as long as you understand the premise on which they're based, you'll find that monitoring them isn't too difficult.

So, let's take a look at straddles first.

Straddles

Unlike spread trades which have a directional bias to them, combination trade strategies are not concerned with the direction the market will move in. All that matters is volatility in these strategies. As such, during any discussion of these strategies you can expect a sprinkling of the so called 'Greeks' which are measures of volatility and other advanced concepts.

However, it is perfectly possible to execute a straddle (or a strangle) even if you're not the world's foremost expert in them. The premise of the straddle is quite simple. You don't care about the direction the market will move in as much as you care about the degree with which it will move.

All the strategies we've looked at thus far have had technical analysis elements to them. In other words, none of them have been purely fundamental in nature. Combination trades can be executed using purely fundamental factors. Things such as special events, macroeconomic releases, earnings announcements, litigation announcements and so on can be used to screen straddle opportunities.

Let's take a look at how the trade is structured.

Trade Structure

The trade consists of two legs. The first is a long put which is close to the money and the second is a long call that is also close to the money. Given that both legs are long, you don't need to worry about the order in which you enter the legs of the trade. What is important is that you make sure the expiration dates of both legs are the same.

The ideal scenario is this. The underlying explodes in a burst of volatility in either direction. By having long options capturing both sides of the market, you are in a good position to benefit no matter what happens. The idea is that the degree by which price will move will be enough to overcome whatever premium you pay to enter the other side of the trade.

This creates a zone around current market price which acts as a profit hurdle for price. As long as price remains within these boundaries, you will not make any money. Hence, there are two things which are extremely important when it comes to straddles. The first is determining the distance at which you want to establish your long option legs.

The second is to determine whether the volatility that you can expect from the underlying checks out. This can be done by looking at the implied volatility of the underlying. As long as it is on the higher side of its historic limits, you can expect significant moves.

How close should your option strike prices be to the market price? There is a tradeoff between volatility and the distance between the strike price and market price here. The lesser the volatility you expect, the closer your strike prices will need to be. However, the closer you get, the higher is the premium you will have to pay to enter the position.

The higher the premium is, the higher is the threshold for price to cross in order for you to make money. Hence, it isn't always a good thing to be as close as possible to market price. Let's look at how this plays out using TSLA as an example.

How it Works

TSLA's current market price is still $478.15. Let's say that earnings season is upon us and analysts are split as to what TSLA's prospects are. Some speculate that if TSLA misses expectations, the company will be in danger of losing even more market share to its competition from the mainstream car industry. They also speculate that if TSLA shows strong earnings growth, this is a great indication that the company is well on track.

As you can expect from such a scenario, you can expect TSLA to increase in price dramatically or decrease equally dramatically. While directional traders will be busy trying to figure out which way the stock is likely to go, you can do the easy thing and simply employ a straddle.

Let's say you choose a long call strike price of $525 and a long-put strike price of $430. The call leg will cost you $15.35 to enter an the put leg will cost you $11.80. Hence, your cost of trade entry is $27.15. This is also the hurdle the price of TSLA has to cross in order to make a profit.

Understand that there are two hurdles here. The first is the hurdle posed by the strike prices. The stock price has to rise or fall to at least the level of the strike prices before you even begin to consider thinking of profits. Next, the premium has to increase by at least $27.15 before you can make a monetary profit. In this case, the rise in intrinsic value should ensure that the option premium will move past the financial hurdle if either option moves into the money.

As far as expiry dates go, you can choose either current month or the month after. Given that the options priced to expire the month after will have the full-time value in them, you're likely to pay a higher price for them.

Thus, it is better to use time decay to your advantage and buy the current month options.

Strangles

Now that you know how straddles work, it's time to take a brief look at strangles. I say brief because strangles are the exact same strategy as straddles. It's just that the option strike prices are further out in anticipation of even greater volatility than with the straddle.

Both trades have the same number of legs to them and rely on the same principles when setting them up. As long as you understand one, executing the other isn't going to be much of an issue.

CHAPTER 11:

Risk and Money Management

The Rhythmic and Cyclical Markets

Ralph Nelson Elliott has developed an approach to interpret wave market movements. His work focuses on hourly Dow Jones quotations and is released from 1938, arousing interest due to the emergence of fractals and chaotic movements.

This analysis considers an alternation between unpredictable periods and deterministic periods. Markets would not be governed by a random walk as Burton Malkiel mentioned. Mandelbrot develops this aspect in his book Fractals, chance, and finance. He considers that the evolution of prices is discontinuous, that prices can shift suddenly, and not in a gradual and continuous way, like good weather and bad weather in short: "If the markets were perfect, they would react instantly to all the news," he exclaimed. Now, they sometimes take time to integrate information and sometimes do so with exaggeration.

Elliott's research leads him to the following conclusion: the continual changes in the stock market reflected a fundamental harmony of nature. Thus, he notes that variations in the Dow Jones Industrial Average (DJIA) construct visible figures that return in the same forms, although they may vary in duration and amplitude.

These observations will allow him to develop a theory, known as Elliott's Wave Theory. It combines the psychological dimension borrowed from Charles Dow and the harmony of nature identified by the mathematician Fibonacci. It consists of a set of empirical rules to interpret the evolution of the main stock indices. This tool is powerful because the rules and principles stated by Elliott are supposed to contain all the action of the market. The main advantage of the Elliott Wave Method is to set up scenarios, set targets and has points of invalidation, the universe of possibilities being known.

This approach is very interesting because it allows one to consider the cyclicality of the financial markets. Indeed, stock prices evolve in a cyclical way: a rise or a fall will never appear in time and will be punctuated by movements of consolidation or correction. Elliott was one of the first writers to highlight the concept of action/reaction which posits that each impulsive movement must be followed by a corrective movement, the impulsive movement being more important in amplitude than the corrective movement.

For example, in an uptrend, the amplitude of impulsive (bullish) waves is generally stronger than that of corrective waves (downs) and vice versa.

During a marked trend, it seems obvious that the market can blow after an impulsive movement. This phenomenon can easily be explained by profit-taking. New entrants (buyers in an uptrend and sellers in a downtrend) are waiting for the presence of a low point to position themselves, which will allow the resumption of the dominant trend. The great strength of Elliott's waves is to be a complete method that emphasizes the two most important elements in trading that are price and time.

Elliott Wave Decomposition

In various articles that were published in the Financial World in 1939, Elliott indicated that the market's bottom rate was a cycle of eight waves, containing five waves of the rise and three waves of decline. The three waves of decline are a correction of the five previous waves of increase.

For Elliott, every impulsive movement is followed by a corrective movement. An impulsive movement is composed of five waves of a lower degree of which three are impulsive and two are corrective. The corrective movement is composed of three waves, two of which are corrective, and one is impulsive.

We will first describe the decomposition of the five waves contained in the impulsive movement:

The first wave represents the arrival of precursors on the markets. The latter anticipates the market turnaround and the imminence of an impulsive movement. They seek to return at the very beginning of the movement and correspond to the initiated investors mentioned by Charles Dow.

The second wave very often corresponds to a strong correction of the first impulsive movement. It represents the entry of contrarians who play the decline because they believe that the market remains in a bearish phase.

The third wave is usually that of followers and professional investors. The news is positive, and the operators are rushing on the title, causing a strong upward acceleration. It's the most powerful impulsive wave, and it's never the shortest.

The fourth wave is profit-taking by operators who took advantage of the sharp rise in a wave. Nevertheless, the trend remains bullish and it is not questioned.

The fifth wave is the last impulsive wave of major impulsive movement. It corresponds to the entry of late followers, who have observed the rise without positioning themselves and who are eager to enjoy the movement like others. Generally, they are the first victims of the market downturn. This wave is also characterized by a depletion of the technical indicators which often draw a bearish divergence and point the breathlessness of the trend in progress and the imminence of a correction.

On many impulsive waves, it is not uncommon to note the presence of an "extension": it is a wave of impulse which is prolonged, and which marks the power of the wave in question. This extension usually takes shape on a single impulsive wave, which allows analysts to take the measure of other waves. Thus, if the first and third waves are of the same length, the fifth will certainly be an extension. The rules set out by Elliott are supposed to contain all the action of the market.

According to Elliott, this decomposition is found whatever the period is chosen. Some analysts do not hesitate to make a comparison with the theory of chaos, developed especially by Mandelbrot. According to this theory, there would be an order in apparent disorder, and images taken at different scales (short term, long term) may have striking similarities. They forget, however, that the principal concerned, Mandelbrot, does not take Elliott's waves seriously. But let us leave aside these sterile quarrels and interest us in the most important: this method is popular, it is followed (the trader must, therefore, integrate it into his arsenal) and it is even sometimes effective!

Four Basic Principles and Five Rules

There are several principles governing Elliott's waves, which we will summarize into basic principles:

Action is followed by a reaction: markets never go up in a single time; the impulse waves, movements in the direction of the primary tendency, break down into five waves of a lower degree, and the corrective waves, movements against the primary trend (bullish or bearish), are decomposed into three waves of a lower degree;

When a movement in eight waves (five up and three down) ends, a complete cycle comes to an end, and this cycle becomes two subdivisions in the immediately higher degree wave; whatever the time horizon, the way of counting is the same because the market is moving at the same pace. The rules stated must imperatively be applied during a count and will be controlled over time.

Corrective Waves

There are several types of corrective waves (zigzags, flats, etc.). In a 5-step movement, corrective waves always correct the previous upward movement. The following properties are the most commonly observed: wave 2 corrects wave 1 and wave 4 corrects wave 3. Elliott, along with several top-flight analysts, noted that corrective waves regularly corrected the impulsive movements of a certain percentage.

Standard Wave Retracement Ratios 2

Wave 2 is often the strongest and corrects waves 1. It traces the previous move at a minimum of 38.2% to 50%, but the standard retracement is 61.8% and can go up to a maximum of 76.4%.

Standard Wave Retracement Ratios 4

Wave 4 represents profit-taking. The correction is never strong and stands at least 23.6%, the standard is 38.2% and they never retrace more than 50%. If the correction is greater than 50% then it is probably necessary to question its count because it is probably a wave 1.

In summary, Wave 2 corrects strongly (61.8% is the standard ratio); while Wave 4 is profit-taking (the standard ratio is often 38.2%).

Can We Distinguish A Corrective Wave from A True Reversal of The Trend?

We have previously seen that an uptrend could be called into question when a lower precedent was depressed. A correction was then drawn, and the prices have depressed the two previous low points without that preventing the title from continuing its ascent. Indeed, this corrective movement corrects the entirety of the previous movement.

The corrective movement corresponds to a true reversal of the trend if and only if the corrective wave sinks the low point of the previous impulsive movement. If not, the current trend remains healthy and nothing comes to question it.

The Rule of Alternation

This rule is a powerful principle of Elliott's waves. The principle is simple: if a wave 2 corrects strongly, then the correction in wave 4 will be weaker. Conversely, if wave 2 corrects weakly, expect an impulsive wave 3 but also a correction in wave 4 powerful.

The second property of alternation rules is based on the simplicity or complexity of the correction. At a wave 2 simple usually follows a complex wave 4. Conversely, if Wave 2 is complex then Wave 4 will be simple.

Impulsive Waves

Impulsive waves are linked together by Fibonacci ratios. Thus, the objective of wave 3 is often obtained in the following way: we multiply the length of the wave 1 by 1.618 and we postpone the result obtained on the bottom of the wave 2. Often, wave 3 will go to hit this objective before correcting in wave 4. But during powerful movements in extension, the ratio will be higher than 1,618. The following ratios are usually taken: 2-2,618-3 and so on.

If wave 2 is weakly traced (less than 50%), expect a powerful wave 3 and project it with ratios above the standard of 1.618.

Advantages

The main advantage of Elliott's method of waves is that it forces the analyst and the trader to imagine different counts, which is an excellent preparation to face the different eventualities.

A good "elliottist" is never closed, and he will always highlight in his analysis a favorite scenario (the one that has the best chance of unfolding) and an alternative (a scenario that would invalidate his ideal scenario).

Disadvantages

The first disadvantage of Elliott waves is the learning time they require. Does the time devoted to training Elliott's waves necessarily find a justification?

I will answer that it may be interesting for a trader to know the basics of Elliott's waves and their fundamentals, but that the signals provided by this method do not seem sufficiently convincing to devote too much time.

The waves of Elliott fascinate many stakeholders, so much so that they become slaves. This method makes it possible to identify turning points with a confusing precision. Nevertheless, the trap of this method of analysis is to force the countdown in a situation where none seems apparent. The analyst then stubbornly searches for movements in five times where there are none.

This danger is well illustrated by the well-known Elliott Wave Advisor Prechter, who became famous in 1987 for predicting the stock market crash with this method. In the 1990s, his market diagnosis was extremely negative, and he hammered in all the media that the US market was about to enter a prolonged bearish phase. This analyst was trapped by his method. He fell in love with it instead of considering it for what it really is: a simple analytical tool.

The moral of this story is two-fold: the markets are always right, and the trader who fights against this reality may pay very dearly.

CHAPTER 12

Analyzing Mood Swings
in the Market

M odern markets are so volatile that a simple buy-and-hold strategy no longer has a place even for the long term.

The Market Is Uptrend

A bullish market is characterized by a succession of lower and higher points, and higher and higher points. In a clear uptrend, the corrective phases (drop legs) are less important in amplitude than the impulsive phases (legs of rising). This property is very important because it provides a valuable indication of the possibility of a trend reversal. When a corrective leg has a greater amplitude than the impulsive leg (bullish in a bull market), then the uptrend is likely to be challenged. The trader will have to reconsider the current trend and avoid positioning himself for the purchase under these conditions.

A downtrend market is characterized by lower and higher points, but also by lower and lower points. In this type of market, rebounds often have less amplitude than bearish legs, the main characteristic of

89

a bear market. In a trending market, the movements that go in the direction of the dominant trend are still the most powerful. As for the uptrend, the turnaround can be anticipated. This requires the recovery to be larger than the last bearish wave.

The Market without Trend

In a trendless market, there is no clear trend, and low points and high points are often confused. Buyers and sellers are testing themselves and no clear consensus is at work.

According to Wilder, markets evolve in trend one-third of the time and do not draw any clear trend during the remaining two-thirds. This property is important because investors are often victims of momentum bias. They tend to mechanically prolong the recent course evolution. If the course progresses during the last sessions, they are convinced of the continuation of its rise and many traders are trapped by positioning themselves around resistance or slightly above2. Conversely, in the case of a decline in stock prices, investors say that this decline will continue and are trapped by opening a position around major support.

The good trader can wait patiently for the right moment before opening a position. Professional traders seek to position themselves at the beginning of an impulsive movement and avoid exposure by taking unnecessary risks when the market is not predictable. Good traders are people who can adapt to changing market conditions. As we will see later, markets fluctuate differently depending on whether we are in an uptrend, bearish trend or a trending market. In a bullish (bearish) market, the trader will be able to afford to buy (sell) up (down) and sell (buy) even higher (low), even if that is not ideal.

Trend Lines

Trend lines are often used by traders to identify bullish points in an uptrend and highs in a downtrend. In a bull market, the trend line goes through at least two low points. Conversely, in a downtrend market, the trend line will join at least two high points. It is possible to adjust trends over time based on new information: sharper, more marked trends may indeed appear as the trend initially traced becomes obsolete.

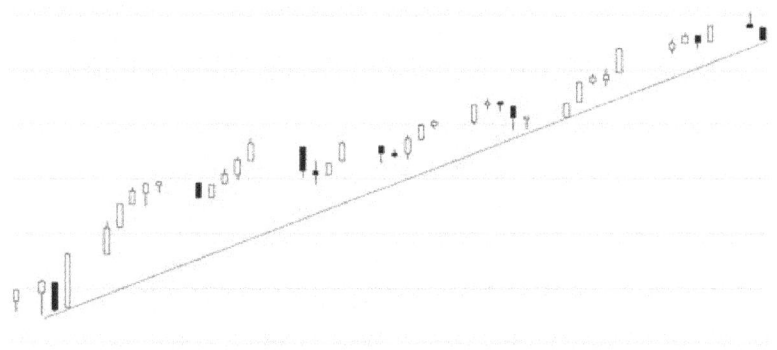

Conditions of Effectiveness of a Trend Line

The success of trend lines is justified by their effectiveness in identifying good levels of support and resistance. In other words, they sometimes make it possible to give with surprising precision these minor levels of reversal when a trend has already started. They also offer the possibility of identifying the state of the trend and anticipating reversals or simply corrective movements. In what follows, we try to give some elements to explain their effectiveness.

A first approach advances the argument of a stock market evolution respecting a "natural" phenomenon. There would exist on the market, and on all time horizons, trends that would respect a speed of progression and therefore a certain angle. The famous trader and analyst WD Gann explain that to last, a trend line must have a 45-degree angle. Not to mention natural phenomenon, we can say that a course of courses with a low slope indicates a slow movement that will probably abort. Conversely, when the slope is steep, the movement is too impulsive and will quickly run out of steam. The ideal is, therefore, to have an average slope (45 degrees), a sign of a healthy impulsive movement.

Another militant element in favor of trend lines is the fact that they are known to most operators. As we have seen, their validity will be strengthened because of the phenomenon of self-fulfilling prophecies. In concrete terms, a bullish trader will draw a trend line to identify the probable drop-off point for the stock, which will be a good buy with low risk. In the opposite case, it will draw a downtrend line to identify sales levels.

The importance of a trend line depends on the number of points it connects. The higher the number of rebounds on the right, the greater the importance. This is explained in particular by the mimicry of operators, which reinforces the strength of this line. In addition, the trend lines can be plotted over several time horizons (long, medium and short term), but the long-term trend lines or just to take them are those whose reliability is the most important. The trader will enjoy a return to the right of support (resistance) to strengthen its position buying (seller) and especially as the quality of the trend is proven.

Finding a Trend Reversal Using a Trend Line

Rupture of a trend line is an important reversal signal. This signal is all the stronger as the trend line is significant (it has been used on many occasions to support the current trend). The break of a bullish or bearish straight line materializes the end of a market dynamic: the operators who should have strengthened their positions near the trend line proved to be weaker than the opposing side (the bearers), thus allowing the rupture of the right and all the dynamics of the market. The change in trend thus seems clear.

A broken bullish straight line immediately becomes a line of resistance against which the market will crash; this is very often shown by a pullback (return to the right of a trend that has just been broken). The market thus tests the strength of the support that has become resistance (or vice versa). Beware; the break of a trend line cannot alone constitute a signal of a reversal of the market, as shown by the example of the title PPR. It only alerts the trader about the possibility of consolidation.

Canals or Channels

A channel (Canal) is a figure directly related to the analysis of trend lines studied previously. The tracking is simple: once a bullish trend has been determined, it is a question of finding a parallel to the tendency to cover all the evolution of prices. Over the period when the trend is observed (straight line connecting the extreme points), we thus obtain a channel in which the courses evolve harmoniously.

The channel will tuck into a trend by allowing impulse turning points to be determined through trend lines, but also corrective turning points through the upper channel of the uptrend channel - or the bottom line for a downtrend channel.

The courses thus vary between these two lines: the first constitutes the support line of the canal, where the courts come to rest; the second represents the resistance line of the channel (or top of the channel) against which the market stumbles.

As for trends, it is possible to distinguish short, medium and long-term channels. The importance of a channel depends on its duration of evolution, but also on the number of times each line of the channel has been affected. To be considered a canal, you need at least two impacts on each side. The higher the number of impacts, the more important the channel is.

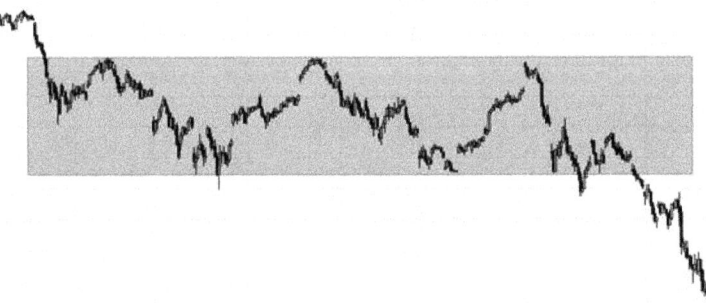

Intermediate Lines

In practice, prices do not move stubbornly between the lower bound and the upper bound. They sometimes have trouble passing intermediate areas within the canal. It is possible to draw parallel straight lines to the channel which constitute as many lines of support or minor resistance for the courses. However, the number of real intermediate rights is limited; one generally finds only one, even two. They are very often halfway through the channel and are real tests to know if the courses will reach the top or bottom. In the case of a bullish channel, the break in the intermediate resistance line often indicates that the market will reach the top of the channel.

It is also possible to distinguish within a channel small intermediate channels that allow, for example, the market to move from one terminal to another. Sometimes, too, a new channel emerges inside the canal, which appears more and more relevant, and which will eventually replace the old one that has become obsolete.

Rupture of the Canal

Two kinds of breaks can be envisaged: either the trend is confirmed and reinforced (it is an upward outflow of the uptrend channel or the decline of a downtrend channel), or it is reversed, and it is then a possible change of trend (downward release of a bullish channel and exit up a downtrend channel). The break is all the stronger as it is done in a large volume.

The operator has several elements to identify a possible rupture of the channel: in the case of a downward exit of a bullish channel, we usually notice that the courses have no strength, they do not arrive for example more to pass the intermediate right but stumble against it regularly. These elements are usually the first alarm signals.

Precautions When Detecting a Signal

The breaking of a bullish channel does not necessarily mean a sell signal, just as the break of a bearish channel does not always correspond to a buy signal. This is a simple indication that will need to be supported by other elements to become a relevant signal.

How to Detect the End of a Trend?

Can trend reversals be identified using chart analysis? We will see that it is possible to plot a reversal graphically, but for this, the trader will have to make sure that several criteria are respected: it is necessary to have a clear trend (for example, a trend line whose impulsive movements have a greater amplitude than corrective movements); the breaking of a major trend line or a major support is often a precursor signal of reversal; and finally, the various researches show that a figure of large turnaround (thus which took some time to be formed) will often be at the origin of an important corrective movement.

The Trend Reversal

After a downward movement (bullish), the title draws a bullish leg (bearish) whose amplitude is greater than the previous bearish (bullish) leg. This configuration signals a probable reversal of the trend and indicates the imminence of a bullish (bearish) departure or simply the cessation of the current trend and the entry of the market in a phase without a trend.

This presentation of trends has been deliberately simplified because, in fact, the range of movements is much richer. Nevertheless, it is important to have a clear idea of the main trends in the markets before refining the analysis. The AGF stock is the typical case of a stock that draws a strong uptrend with very few corrections. It was difficult for a buyer to find a low point allowing him to position himself in the direction of the trend.

How Are Trends Formed?

Trends are a common phenomenon in the markets, but their training is often misunderstood by operators. Dow has developed a theory to provide relevant explanations for this phenomenon and can usefully be applied to current markets, regardless of the period used.

CHAPTER 13:

Brokers

When it comes to selecting brokers, you have many options available. There are full service, discount, online, etc. Understanding the differences between them and selecting the ones best suited for your purposes is crucial if you wish to succeed. Another area that a lot of beginners ignore and then receive a rude lesson in is the regulations surrounding options trading.

There aren't too many rules to comply with, but they do have significant consequences for your capital and risk strategies.

Choosing a Broker

Generally speaking, there are two major varieties of brokers: Discount and full service. In fact, a lot of full-service brokers have discount arms these days so you will see some overlap. Full service refers to an organization where brokerage is just a part of a larger financial supermarket.

The broker might offer you other investment solutions, estate planning strategies, and so on. They'll also have an in-house research wing which will send you reports to help you trade better. In addition to this, they'll also have phone support in case you have any questions or wish to place an order.

Once you develop a good relationship with them, a full-service broker will become a good organization to network. Every broker loves a profitable customer since it helps with marketing. A full-service broker will have good relationships in the industry and if you have specific needs, they can put you in touch with the right people.

The price of all this service is you paying higher commissions than average. It is up to you to see whether this is a good price for you to pay. As such, you don't need to sign up with a full-service broker to trade successfully.

Order matching is done electronically so it's not as if a person on the floor can get you a better price these days. Therefore, a full-service house is not going to give you better execution.

Discount brokers, on the other hand, are all about focus. They help you trade, and that is it. They will not provide advice, at least not intentionally from a business perspective, and phone ordering is nonexistent. That doesn't mean customer service is reduced. Far from it.

Commissions will be lower as well, far lower than what you can expect to pay at a full-service house.

The downside of a discount brokerage is that you're not going to receive any special product recommendations or solutions outside of your speculative activities. A lot of people prefer to trade (using a separate account) with the broker they have their retirement accounts with, so everything is kept in-house.

So, which one should you choose? Well, if you aim to keep costs as low as possible, then select a discount broker. In fact, only in the case where you're keen on keeping things in one place should you choose a full-service broker. These days, there's no difference between the two options otherwise.

Margin

Margin refers to the number of assets you currently hold in your account. Your assets are cash and positions. As the market value of your positions fluctuates, so does the amount of margin you have. Margin is an important concept to grasp since it is at the core of your risk management discipline.

When you open an account with your broker, you will have a choice to make. You can open either a cash or margin account. In order to trade options, you have to open a margin account. Briefly, a cash account does not include leverage within it, so all you can trade are stocks. There are no account minimums for a cash account, and even if they are, they're pretty minuscule.

A margin account, on the other hand, is subject to very different rules. First, the minimum balances for a margin account are higher. Most brokers will impose a $10,000 minimum, and some will even increase this amount based on your trading style. The account minimum doesn't achieve anything by itself, but it acts as a commitment of sorts for the broker.

The thinking is that with this much money on the line, the person trading is going to be a bit more serious about it and won't blow it away. If only it worked like that. Anyway, the minimum balance is a hard and fast rule. Another rule you should be aware of is the Pattern Day Trader (PDT) designation.

PDT is a rule that comes directly from the SEC. Anyone who executes four or more orders within five days is classified as a PDT ("Pattern Day Trader," 2019). One this tag is slapped onto you; your broker is going to ask you to post at least $25,000 in the margin as a minimum balance. Again, this minimum balance doesn't do anything but the SEC figures that if you do screw up, this gives you enough of a buffer.

Will the strategies in this book get you classified as a PDT? Well, this depends on you. Each strategy by itself plays out over a month or more so once you enter, all you need to do is monitor it and if you want, you can adjust it. However, if you're going to avoid the PDT, you're limited to entering just three positions per workweek.

My advice is to study the strategies and to start slowly. Trade just one instrument at first and see how it goes and then expand once you gain more confidence. At that point, you'll have enough experience to figure out how much capital you need. Remember that even exiting a position is considered a trade, so PDT doesn't refer just to trade entry.

Margin Call

One other aspect of margin you must understand is the margin call. This is a dreaded message for most traders, including institutional ones. The purpose of all risk management is to keep you as far away as possible from this ever happening to you. A margin call is issued when you have inadequate funds in your account to cover its requirements.

Remember that your margin is the combination of the cash you hold plus the value of your positions. If you have $1000 in cash, but your position is currently in a loss of -$900, you'll receive a margin call to post more cash to cover the potential loss you're headed for. In fact, you'll receive it well in advance. If you don't post more margin, your broker has the right to close out your positions and recover whatever cash they can to stop their risk limits from being triggered.

The threshold beyond which your broker will issue a margin call is called the maintenance margin. Usually, you need to maintain 25% of your initial position value (that is when you enter a position) as cash in your account. Most brokers have a handy indicator which tells you how close you are to the limit.

The leading cause of margin calls is leverage. With a margin account, you can borrow money from your broker and use that to boost your returns. Let's look at an example: if you trade with $10,000 of your own money and borrow $20,000 from your broker to enter a position, you control $30,000 worth of the position.

Let's say this position makes a gain of $10,000 to bring its total value to $40,000.

You've just made a 100% return on this investment (since you invested just $10,000) despite the total return on the position is 33% (10,000/30,000). What happens if you lose $10,000 on the position though? Well, you just lost 100% despite the position losing only 33%. Leverage is a double-edged sword. It is far too simplistic to call leverage bad or good. It is what it is. If you're a beginner, you should not be borrowing money to trade under any circumstances. When you're experienced, you can choose to do so as much as you want. Please note, I'm differentiating between the leverage where you borrow money, and the sort of leverage options provide. With options, a single contract gives you control over a larger pie of stock, but the option premium still needs to be paid. It is, therefore, cheaper to trade options than the common stock. If you were to borrow money to pay for the option premium, then you're indulging in foolish behavior, and you need to step away. There's a difference between leverage being inherent within the structure of the instrument and using leverage to increase the amount of something you can buy. The latter should be avoided when you're a beginner.

Execution

A favorite pastime of unsuccessful traders is to complain about execution. Their losses are always the broker's fault, and if it weren't for the greedy brokers, they'd be rolling in the dough, diving in and out of it like Scrooge McDuck. Complaining about your execution will get you nothing. A big reason for these complaints is that most beginner traders don't realize that the price they see on the screen is not the same as what is being traded on the exchange.

We live in an era of high-frequency trading, and the markets' smallest measurement of time has gone from seconds to microseconds. Trades are constantly pouring in, and the matching engine is always finding suitable sellers for buyers. Given the pace of the market, it is important to understand that it is humanly impossible to figure out the exact price of an instrument.

Therefore, within your risk management plan, you must make allowance for times of high volatility when the fluctuations will be bigger. For now, I want you to understand that just because the price you received was different from what was on screen doesn't mean the broker is incompetent.

How do you identify an incompetent broker? Customer service and the quality of the trading terminal they give you access to are the best indicators. Your broker is not in the game to trade against you or fleece you. Admittedly, this is not the case with FX, but we're not discussing FX in this book. So, stop blaming your broker and look at your systems instead, assuming the broker passes basic due diligence.

Price Quotes

A lot of traders are stumped when they first look at their trading screens and see that there are two prices for everything. After all, every financial channel always displays one price for security but when trading, you'll be quoted two different prices within the price box. This is a small but crucial detail for you to understand.

The lower price you receive is called the bid, and this is the price you will pay if you sell the instrument. The higher price is the ask, and this is what you will pay to buy the instrument. The single price you see on your TV screen is the "Last Traded Price" or LTP. Do not make the mistake of thinking the LTP is the real price since the market moves constantly.

In fact, even the spread (the difference between the ask and the bid) doesn't accurately reflect the true state of things thanks to constant movement. There's no need to be alarmed though, as long as volatility is stable, the difference isn't much. Just remember to look at the spread to understand what you'll be paying. The spread increases and contracts constantly but if you see that it is getting too big, this is a sign that too much volatility exists and you're better off staying out.

This concludes our look at brokers and the ins and outs of it. As you can see, there isn't too much to be concerned about, but you need to be well aware since it impacts how much capital you'll be trading with. Generally speaking, the higher the capital you have, the safer you'll be since you'll have more room to make mistakes.

CHAPTER 14:

Technical Analysis and Its Basics

No matter the kind of vehicle you choose for your actions, there are some basics that you have to be familiar with. This fundamental knowledge is mostly connected to the behavior of the markets. If you learn how to recognize the way they behave, you will be able to anticipate the movement of the prices more accurately, thus make smarter decisions while trading. It can be interesting to note that regardless of the value that is traded on the market, some concepts can always apply to the prices and their way of performance on the market.

This can be explained by independent traders and investors being responsible for short-term price fluctuations. We can say that the price depends on the actions of the people who invest or trade values on the market and that prices react in a similar way when they are given similar input or stimuli. The study that is dedicated to researching the ways of price behavior is called technical analysis and understanding its basic is one of the most essential education points that you will need to be able to make correct financial decisions on the market.

The basics of Technical Analysis

Technical analysis represents a huge topic. If you decide to enter the market and become an investor, there is a high possibility that you will catch yourself coming back to studying and learning something new many times for as long as you intend to work as a trader. That is why every person knowledgeable in options trading would advise that a basic understanding of technical analysis is a very important step for every person involved in the market. However, you don't need to know everything about it right away. Since it is a large area of research, it is ok if for some aspects of your business you just research parts of the technical analysis that you are particularly interested in for that concrete project. For instance, the technical analysis offers more than a hundred indicators for analyzing the market. In reality, traders usually use three or four, mostly the most popular ones or just those that they were familiar within the first place. If you don't limit yourself only to option trading but you do trade in general, you will realize that technical analysis can be applied to any financial instruments such as futures or stocks for example. We can say that their basis is in psychology and human nature in general and how they behave in practice. For better understanding, we will overview some of the main topics in technical analysis. These topics will be:

Technical analysis' foundation; how to chart principles and trends; patterns in technical analysis; technical analysis through the movement of the averages, and Indicators in technical analysis.

Technical analysis' foundation

The main basis of the technical analysis is found in the term known as '' market action". Market action represents a whole personal knowledge about the trading market, and it doesn't include information that you might obtain from an insider. It can be simply defined as a study that determines: ''the way that the price moves over time". If possible, it also examines its volumes and how they change over time too.

Still, the fundamental concept of technical analysis is based on the premise that the behavior of the market is a reflection of everything that happened and will happen with the price at a certain moment. Many things can have an impact on the price, and the amount of the impact depends on the market in which the trade is made. That's where technical analysis comes in, it cuts across all of those possibilities and states that all the things that can be known about the price are basically already included in the price that we see at the moment we want to trade.

This means that you shouldn't worry too much about the things that influence the price, as according to this it is enough to follow how the price changes over time and you will get all your answers. At first, many people wondered if this kind of principle can work because it sounded rather easy. If you had any doubts, the answer was already proven and it says that yes, technical analysis is successful although this kind of definition doesn't seem that complicated.

However, there is one very important point coming out from all of this. Technical analysis doesn't guarantee the behavior of the price. It can tell you that the price will increase or decrease for a certain period, but that doesn't necessarily happen. It may or it may not. The reason for this is that regardless of the calculation that the market has to do something, it is impossible to be 100 percent sure that it will. The market has its own ways and eventually does what it wants. So what technical analysis does is that it gives you the indication that shows what will be the most probable outcome, which means that the only certainty that you get is to know if the law of probability is on your side or not.

You can do a large number of average trades and hopefully make some profit, but you should never invest an amount of money or some valuable goods such as your house or your car if you can't afford to lose it. It is not recommended especially if one successful trade makes you confident that just one is enough to be a good technical indicator for certain gain. This is one of the reasons why the first task of technical analysis is to improve your chance for success by analyzing the prices and the way they behave on the market.

The second reason for the analysis is the fact that prices almost always change using certain trends. For instance, if the price increases its trend will be to rise until there is something that disables it from further growth. In comparison, we can say that prices act like Newton's motion law, which says that: ''a body in motion will stay in motion unless acted upon by an external force." Of course, to prove this to be true, it has to happen over time. If this wasn't the case the price charts represented in many analyses wouldn't be the way they are. They would be illustrated as a random movement of the prices. The third reason is that technical analysis supposes that history will, as always, repeat itself. If certain situations happened in the past, and you see them happening once again in the present than it is highly expected that the same thing will happen in the future too. Since people are not expected to change in this equation, the second logical conclusion would be that their results will be the same too. In a nutshell- this was a very foundation of technical analysis. Don't forget that one of the most efficient ways to become good in trading and to increase your chance to become a successful investor is to be able to use most of the things that this analysis can give you.

There are a few arguments that you can hear against the use of technical analysis. Still, the only proof that you really need is the fact that this analysis works and that at least it can improve your chances to get more percentages while trading. However, we will point out some of the attitudes toward technical analysis:

One of the traders said: ''Charts only show what has happened in the past, how they can reveal what hasn't happened yet?'' The answer to this is quite simple, there is evidence from earlier trades and those pieces of evidence are used in technical analysis with the premise that history will repeat itself. This way you can anticipate at least with some fair certainty what is the next thing that will happen with the price on the market. In comparison, it works in a similar way as the weather forecast, if they say that it will rain on the TV, you know that it might not rain even though they said it will, but you take your umbrella with you anyway. The same principle applies with the technical analysis and that is how you can predict the future by using the past events.

Another trader noted: ''If the prices already incorporate everything there is to know, then any change in price can only come from new information that we don't know yet.'' This kind of idea doesn't only appear in trading options, it is present in all financial markets. It surfaces in many areas and even academics are still discussing it. Differently, from the opinion that is popular between the traders, this concept doesn't actually say that the price that is currently on the market is the correct one. It just states that it isn't possible to establish if that current price is too low or too high. That is why the smartest choice to deal with this concept is to prove in which way technical analysis really works. In the end, if everyone supported this kind of idea then we would have zero analysis and the price would be always the same. We can imply that technical analysis has self-fulfilling characteristics.

This means that if the majority of traders do the analysis and estimate that the price has to increase all of them would become buyers on the market, which would mean an increase in demand, thus price that went up. The same principle applies to the price that

113

is supposed to go down. This is one more example in which technical analysis showed that it works. Of course, there can always be some doubts, but does it really matter to prove why the price went in the direction that you thought it would? Additionally, if a large number of traders who are not well educated and they just want to make quick profit fail, it can be seen as a sort of evidence that the idea of having a massive amount of traders regardless of their knowledge and dedication is somehow wrong from the beginning.

CHAPTER 15:

The Greeks

Attempting to assume what happens to a particular option's price or a scenario with multiple options amid changes in the market can be quite an undertaking. Since the price of an option is not always dictated by the underlying asset's price, understanding contributing factors to an option price's movement and the corresponding effects is a useful skill in options trading.

Finding the Values

First, keep in mind that the numbers assigned to Greeks should be considered as strictly theoretical. These values are computer-based on certain mathematical models. Most of the data required to trading options, such as open interest, volume, last prices, ask, and bid, is data extracted from facts received from different options exchanges that are distributed by the brokerage firm and/or data service.

Greeks should be computed, and accuracy is highly dependent on the model that was used to calculate them. Getting them requires access to computerized solutions that compute them as per your request. Most interactive brokers or retail brokerages also give out this data. It is possible, however, to learn the underlying math and compute for the Greeks manually, but given the time constraints and the number of available options, it's impractical and unrealistic.

The Delta

Most options trading beginners fall into the assumption that if a certain stock moves by a dollar, the options price based on it is going to move more than a dollar. If you think about it, this belief is rather silly. Remember that the option is always priced lower than the stock so there is no logical reason to reap more benefit compared to owning the stock itself.

Having realistic expectations regarding the price behaviors of the traded options is essential. The real question now is, if a stock moves by $1, how much is the price of that option going to move? This is where 'delta' comes in.

Calls have what is called positive delta with a value between zero and one. So, when the price of a stock goes up and there are no changes in other pricing variables, the call's price will also go up. For example, when a call has a set delta of 0.50 and stock moves up by $1, theoretically, the call's prices will also go up by about $0.50.

As a rule of thumb, 'in the money' options will always move more than its counterpart 'out of the money' options. Also, short-term options always react more than options that are longer-term to the same stock price change.

As the expiration nears, delta value for 'in the money' puts also nears -1 and delta value for 'out of the money' puts will near 0. This is because when puts are locked until the expiration, the owner should either choose to exercise the options then sell the stock or the put becomes worthless when it expires.

Thinking About Delta Differently

What we have explained previously is delta's textbook definition. However, you can think about delta in a different but useful way – the possibility that an option will end up at least $0.01 'in the money' when it expires.

This may not be a valid technical definition of delta since the math behind it is not considered standard probability calculation. However, the delta is often used similarly with probability in the world of options trading.

In casual options trading lingo, dropping the decimal point in delta figures is a common practice. So, you might hear someone saying, 'That guy's option has a delta of 60'. Or, 'When I finish this e-book, there's a 99 delta that I'm treating myself to a beer'.

An 'at the money' call option will usually have a delta around 0.50, or simply '50 delta'. This is because there's a 50/50 chance this option will end up either 'in the money' or 'out of the money' when it expires. Now let's discuss how the delta value starts to change as the option gets further 'in the money' or 'out of the money'.

How Delta Is Affected by the Movement of Stock Price

As a certain option goes further 'in the money', the possibility that it will end up 'in the money' when it expires also increases. This means the delta of the option also increases. Vice versa, as the option goes further 'out of the money', the possibility that it will end up 'in the money' when it expires also decreases. So, the delta of the option will decrease.

For example, you currently have a call option for stock ABC with a $50 strike price, and the price of the stock is $50, 60 days before expiration. Because this is an 'at the money' option, the delta is around 0.50. Let's say your option is priced at $2. Theoretically, when the price of the stock changes to $51, the price of the option also goes up to $2.50 from the original $2.

What if the price of this stock goes up to $52 from $51? Now, the probability that the option winds up 'in the money' when it expires is also higher. So, what happens to delta? If you're thinking that the delta increases, you're correct.

Let's apply the principle in our example. If the price of the stock goes up to $52 from $51, the price of the option might also go up to $3.10 from $2.50, which is a $0.60 move for the stock's $1 movement. This means delta increased from 0.50 to 0.60 ($3.10 minus $2.50 equals $0.60), as that stock went further 'in the money'.

But what if instead of going up, the price of the stock goes down to $49 from $50? The price of the option might also go down to $1.50 from $2, which again reflects the delta of 0.50 for the 'at the money options' ($2 minus $1.50 equals $0.50. But if the price of the stock goes down further to $48, the price of the option might also go down to $1.10 from $1.50. In this case, delta went down to 0.40 ($1.50 minus $1.10 equals $0.40). This delta decrease means that the probability the option ends up 'in the money' when it expires is also lower.

How Delta Is Affected as Expiration Nears

Similar to the price of the stock, the probability wherein options will wind up 'in the money' or 'out of the money' is affected by the time until expiration. This is because as the expiration nears, there is less time for the stock to move below or above the strike price of the option.

Because probabilities will change as expiration nears, delta reacts differently to stock price changes. If the calls are 'in the money' just before the expiration, delta will get near an almost 1 value and that option moves penny-for-penny together with the stock. On the other hand, puts that are 'in the money' will get near -1 as expiration approaches.

If the option is 'out of the money', it will get near 0 faster than it would with more time. It will also stop reacting to the stock's movement.

Let's have a similar example we had earlier. You have stock ABC priced at $50, and the option to call for the $50 strike price is only a day away from expiration. The data, as usual, is about 0.50, because there's a theoretical 50/50 chance the stock will move in either direction. What happens when the stock moves up to $51?

Think about the scenario. If the expiration is only a day away with the option a point 'in the money', what might be the probability that the option remains at least $0.01 'in the money' tomorrow? If you're thinking it's quite high, you're correct.This is because delta increases accordingly, making a grand move to 0.90 from 0.50. Conversely, when stock ABC goes down to $49 from $50 a mere day before the expiration date of the option, delta might go down to 0.10 from 0.50, because of the decreased probability the option ends up 'in the money'.

Therefore, as expiration nears, stock value changes will also cause more significant changes in the delta, because of the decreased or increased probability of ending up 'in the money'.

Final Thoughts About Delta

Gamma

Delta is to speed as to gamma is to acceleration. Remember this analogy to understand gamma and its relation to delta better. Gamma is defined as the rate at which delta changes based on a change of $1 on the price of the stock. Options that have high gamma responds the most to movements in the underlying stock's price.

The delta is a moving amount that changes with the stock price. But delta doesn't necessarily change following the same rate of each option based on a certain stock. Let's go back to our stock ABC example having a $50 strike price, to learn how gamma exhibits change in delta with stock price changes and the time until it expires. Take a look at the table above, notice how gamma and delta change when the price of the stock will go North and South starting at $50 with the option moving 'in the money' or 'out of the money'. You will see that the 'at the money' options price change more dramatically compared to 'in the money' or 'out of the money' options price given a similar expiration. Also, near-term 'in the money' options price changes more dramatically compared to longer-term 'at the money' option price. This discussion around gamma shows that near-term 'at the money' options price will reflect the most dramatic response to stock price changes.

Theta

Theta, also called time decay, is the number one enemy for option buyers. Conversely, theta is the seller's best friend. Theta is defined as the amount puts and calls prices theoretically decrease for a single day change within the expiration time.

The graph above shows how the value of an option that's 'at the money' is going to decay in three months until it expires. Notice how the time value decreases at a rate that accelerates as expiration nears. Passage of time in the options market is like the effect of summer's heat on an ice cube. As each moment passes, the time value of the option melts away. And it does not melt away in a linear value. As expiration nears, the rate of this decrease gets faster. Looking at the graph again, you will see that a 90-day option that is 'at the money' and with a $1.70 premium is going to lose $0.30 of its original value in 30 days. If the option has an expiration of 60 days, however, it's value might decrease by $0.40 after 30 days. The 30-day option, on the other hand, is going to lose the whole-time value of $1 when it expires.

Vega

Vega is viewed by traders as the over-excited Greek in the lot. It is defined as the amount put and call prices will move, theoretically, for a corresponding change of one implied volatility point. Vega doesn't affect the options' intrinsic values. It only affects the 'time value' of the price of an option. When there is an increase in implied volatility, there will also be an increase in the options' value since as implied volatility increases, it can also suggest an increased range of the stocks' potential movement.

How About Rho?

Veteran option traders talk about one more Greek – rho. It is defined as the amount the value of an option is going to change, theoretically, based on an interest rate change of once percentage-point.

But as mentioned, this Greek is for the more advanced traders. If you play this game long enough, you might get to meet him.

CHAPTER 16:

Tools and Rules of Options Trading

The Tools Used in Option Trading

Stash: The best app for beginner level trading for their investment decisions. It is a trading and investment app. This is the best choice for your needs. Stash charges $5 to start investing, it offers assistance in what to invest and gives you more information on your investments. The app also has essential articles and tips to help you improve your investment knowledge. Your finances go into single stocks and ETF's, which are incorporated into different investment themes. Stash also has a built-in investment coach.

Stockpile: With Stockpile, you will be able to buy and sell stocks. You can also gift single shares or buy a part of the shares with a minimum of 99-cent trade fees. Using your account, you can be able to purchase high-valued stocks like Google, and Amazon using the fractional trades. And you won't have to pay $1,000 or even more per share. You will also have the option of buying a portion of stock for the lower cost of your investment. Stockpile is very suitable for families because of the buying and gifting shares of a stock feature. Kids, teenagers, and the whole family can have portfolios and can be able to teach your family the importance of investing, and this can become a family activity. Teach your children about money and investment at an early stage and buy shares or gift them with some stocks. By engaging them, they will be able to grow a valued portfolio.

Charles Schwab: The app enables you to manage your investment and also bank accounts all in one app. Schwab also has a feature to allow you to transfer funds, deposit your checks, and manage your finances. You are also able to buy and sell stocks, ETFs, and mutual funds. Schwab is a favorite with international travelers because it offers a checking ATM card whenever the travel with no extra fees. Schwab is user-friendly; you can log in to your Android, Apple, and Kindle fire devices to check your investments. You can also pay bills on the app.

TD Ameritrade: The app is very user-friendly and straightforward to navigate. It is suitable for new option traders. TD Ameritrade offers 24/7 access to customer support via the phone and also through email support. The user can also visit their many local branches to get assistance, and the service can provide research to their users. TD Ameritrade has no hidden charges, and it does not charge platform fees, and also there is no minimum trade fee. The app charges a flat-rate commission of $6.95 equity trade and $0.75 per contract.

TradeStation Mobile: This app is one of the high rated apps, and it is free for all TradeStation clients. The users can see different options contracts with different prices and expiration dates. TradeStation app offers up-to-date information which the traders can access, and they can run options analysis, and also, the traders can view charts with various technical indicators. The app has notification features, and the traders can monitor the price changes and other indicators. TradeStation is a full-service trading app that offers access to stocks, futures options, and also forex trading.

The Rules Used in Option Trading

What are the guidelines to follow in options trading? What are the rules? These are essential questions new traders should be able to answer correctly. In this book, we will go through the rules that you should follow in options trading. And by the end of this topic, you will have the knowledge needed to trade efficiently. For a new emerging trader, these rules will be an eye-opener, while for an experienced options trader, it will be as a reminder. These rules won't be a get-rich tip, and the rules will help you stay out of trouble, increase your capital, and improve your money with options. Here are some of the rules used on options trading:

1. Trade small positions. When you get into the market, it's obvious to assume the worse. It only makes sense to make smaller trades and avoid big trades to reduce the risk of losing a significant

amount of the money you had invested. The best tip is to make lots of small positions because if you make just one large, you risk being knocked out when you hit a loss. About 90% of options traders do not succeed because they trade large position sizes. Trading over 5% is considered a large position, and the trader risk affecting their accounts from a bad loss.

2. Don't be emotional. The market doesn't care what you think; one of the ways to be successful in trading is not to be emotional. Don't allow your emotions to lead you, the opinions or thoughts on the market.

3. Have a high trade count. By knowing your estimated percentage chance of success, you will make a lot of trades. The higher the trade count, the higher the chances of leveling out at that expected percentage. Options trading is a number game and math, and you can pinpoint your probabilities of success in a given position. You can see your percentage chance of success; however, this can be the reason for your failure as you will have the same expectation in all your trades. So, the high trade count you make, the more consistent your percentage success rate will be.

4. Balance your portfolio. You can bet the price direction if it goes up or down when you invest in options trading. Traders tend to focus on the investment value going up; however, you have

to learn how to balance your portfolio with positions going down too.

5. Trade according to your comfort level. If you are not comfortable trading naked options or if hedged positions give you sleepless nights, then you should trade options as a speculator forming opinions and act on them accordingly. Once you are in tune with your strategies, you will realize it will be much easier for you to make money. Each strategy is unique and individual, and it might not work for all traders. By doing this, you will lower the individual's risk level.

6. Always use a model. Failure to check the fair value of the option before it's sold or bought is one of the biggest mistakes option traders make. It can be hard, especially if you don't have an exact real-time evaluation capability. These are the basis of the strategic investment and also be aware of the bargains and the amount you are paying for the option.

7. Have enough cash reserve. It's essential to have a lot of your investment money in cash. It might be useful for brokers as they need a margin requirement when trading. They partition some amount to cover potential losses on your position. Try to keep about 50-60% of your investment portfolio in cash.

8. Reduce commissions and fees. Paying commissions and fees to transact and rebalance your portfolio might be crippling you. One of the

ways to lower the percentage of the charges is by using low-cost ETF's. But for a beginner, you shouldn't pay any fees to invest in stocks.

Ten Commandments of Option Trading

One of the advantages of options trading is that you only lose what you paid for the options. However, no loss, even a smaller one, is fun. Being able to manage a loss is one of the critical keys to making money and becoming more successful in options trading. Here are ten commandments of options trading that can help you improve your options trading in the market:

1. Start with simple transactions. If you started trading in derivatives, it's unwise to get into significant option strategies. Start small with simple trades like buying and selling stock futures. Once you become more experienced with these basic future transactions, you will slowly begin buying call and put options. You have to be an informed investor to be able to start writing of call and put options.

2. Understand the benefits. Examine future and options in a proper outlook. If you trade short in the cash market, you will have to balance off position on that day. But if it's the future, you can move forward in the short position until expiration.

3. Stops loss is a must. Most traders fail in their positions, and they never stick to the

recommended stop loss. When you follow stop losses, you limit the loss if the market goes against you. Any investor who is taking a position in the Options market should abide by the recommended stop loss.

4. The brokerage myth. Low brokerage services don't always result in enormous profits. However, cheap services have low quality in the recommendations, and it leads to weak returns after some time. Good quality is seen in the ideas with significant research. The excellent quality is expensive with a high brokerage, but it's worth it because it will bring considerable returns in the long term.

5. Don't panic when in loss. It's normal for investors to panic when they make a loss in the market. However, the options market offers enough flexibility to help you out when you are stuck in most situations. The market is tense by nature but if you have a confident advisor can help you reduce the risk of losing your investment. Here are some tips option traders can use to keep their emotions in check:

Big picture - to be mindful of the macroeconomic and avoiding overpriced assets.

Always have a plan for your trade - to eliminate any emotions when buying or selling.

Prefer bargains - look for undervalued bargains instead of overpaying.

6. Profit is what you book. Most investors get greedy in the market, mostly in F&O. It's essential that investors avoid getting too greedy and book profits when they achieve their target return. It makes sense to book profits twice than waiting too long. What you book in the market is your profit.

7. Assured return is dead. Investors should avoid looking for a guaranteed return in the Options market. It's vital to understand the options market offers benefits of the cash market with more advantages, but it's not a risk-free product.

8. Stick to one trading methodology. Each brokerage house follows and has its own research methods, which are very different from another brokerage. An investor needs to stick to one brokerage house to get a sustainable return.

9. Get Familiar with the terms. Without knowing the terms used in options, trading will be like flying a plane without reading the instruments. There are important insights available into the sensitivity of options costs changes in the underlying shares, making it essential in risk management. An options trader should try and familiarize themselves with the basic's terms used like:

Delta: This measures the rate of changes in parallel to the cost rate in the stock. For example, the pricing value.

Vega: This measures the sensitive options to volatility, For example, the volatility value.

Theta: This measures the sensitive options on a specific period, also called the option's time decay, for example, a time value.

10.   Plan the trade, trade the plan. The term the disposition effect is where the investors sell their winnings too early, and they keep the losses too long; this is very common. The causes of the results are not known, but options traders can prevent this by having a plan before they start trading and executing the plan without compromising. Here are some steps you can take in planning and executing trades:

CHAPTER 17:

Tips for Success

Know when to go off book: While sticking to your plan, even when your emotions are telling you to ignore it, is the mark of a successful trader, this in no way means that you must blindly follow your plan 100 percent of the time. You will, without a doubt, find yourself in a situation from time to time where your plan is going to be rendered completely useless by something outside of your control. You need to be aware enough of your plan's weaknesses, as well as changing market conditions, to know when following your predetermined course of action is going to lead to failure instead of success. Knowing when the situation really is changing, versus when your emotions are trying to hold sway is something that will come with practice, but even being aware of the disparity is a huge step in the right direction.

Avoid trades that are out of the money: While there are a few strategies out there that make it a point of picking up options that are currently out of the money, you can rest assured that they are most certainly the exception, not the rule. Remember, the options market is not like the traditional stock market which means that even if you are trading options based on underlying stocks buying low and selling high is just not a viable strategy. If a call has dropped out of the money, there is generally less than a 10 percent chance that it will return to acceptable levels before it expires which means that if you purchase these types of options what you are doing is little better than gambling, and you can find ways to gamble with odds in your favor of much higher than 10 percent.

Avoid hanging on too tightly to your starter strategy: Your core trading strategy is one that should always be constantly evolving as the circumstances surrounding your trading habits change and evolve as well. What's more, outside of your primary strategy you are going to want to eventually create additional plans that are more specifically tailored to various market states or specific strategies that are only useful in a narrow band of situations. Remember, the more prepared you are prior to starting a day's worth of trading, the greater your overall profit level is likely to be, it is as simple as that.

Utilize the spread: If you are not entirely risk averse, then when it comes to taking advantage of volatile trades the best thing to do is utilize a spread as a way of both safeguarding your existing investments and, at the same time, making a profit. To utilize a long spread, you are going to want to generate a call and a put, both with the same underlying asset, expiration details, and share amounts but with two very different strike prices. The call will need to have a higher strike price and will mark the upper limit of your profits and the put will have a lower strike price that will mark the lower limit of your losses. When creating a spread, it is important that you purchase both halves at the same time as doing it in fits and spurts can add extraneous variables to the formula that are difficult to adjust for properly.

Never proceed without knowing the mood of the market: While using a personalized trading plan is always the right choice, having one doesn't change the fact that it is extremely important to consider the mood of the market before moving forward with the day's trades. First and foremost, it is important to keep in mind that the collective will of all of the traders who are currently participating in the market is just as much as a force as anything that is more concrete, including market news. In fact, even if companies release good news to various outlets and the news is not quite as good as everyone was anticipating it to be then related prices can still decrease.

To get a good idea of what the current mood of the market is like, you are going to want to know the average daily numbers that are common for your market and be on the lookout for them to start dropping sharply. While a day or two of major fluctuation can be completely normal, anything longer than that is a sure sign that something is up. Additionally, you will always want to be aware of what the major players in your market are up to.

Never get started without a clear plan for entry and exit: While finding your first set of entry/exit points can be difficult without experience to guide you, it is extremely important that you have them locked down prior to starting trading, even if the stakes are relatively low. Unless you are extremely lucky, starting without a clear idea of the playing field is going to do little but lose your money. If you aren't sure about what limits you should set, start with a generalized pair of points and work to fine tune it from there.

More important than setting entry and exit points, however, is using them, even when there is still the appearance of money on the table. One of the biggest hurdles that new options traders need to get over is the idea that you need to wring every last cent out of each and every successful trade. The fact of the matter is that, as long as you have a profitable trading plan, then there will always be more profitable trades in the future which means that instead of worrying about a small extra profit you should be more concerned with protecting the profit that the trade has already netted you. While you may occasionally make some extra profit ignoring this advice, odds are you will lose far more than you gain as profits peak unexpectedly and begin dropping again before you can effectively pull the trigger. If you are still having a hard time with this concept, consider this: options trading is a marathon, not a sprint, slow and steady will always win the race.

Never double down: When they are caught up in the heat of the moment, many new options traders will find themselves in a scenario where the best way to recoup a serious loss is to double down on the underlying stock in question at its newest, significantly lowered, price in an effort to make a profit under the assumption that things are going to turn around and then continue to do so to the point that everything is completely profitable once again. While it can be difficult to let an underlying stock that was once extremely profitable go, doubling down is rarely if ever going to be the correct decision. If you find yourself in a spot where you don't know if the trade you are about to make is actually going to be a good choice, all you need to do is ask yourself if you would make the same one if you were going into the situation blind, the answer should tell you all you need to know.

If you find yourself in a moment where doubling down seems like the right choice, you are going to need to have the strength to talk yourself back down off of that investing ledge and to cut your losses as thoroughly as possible given the current situation. The sooner you cut your losses and move on from the trade that ended poorly, the sooner you can start putting energy and investments into a trade that still has the potential to make you a profit.

Never take anything personally: It is human nature to build stories around, and therefore form relationships with, all manner of inanimate objects including individual stocks or currency pairs. This is why it is perfectly natural to feel a closer connection to particular trades, and possibly even consider throwing out your plan when one of them takes an unexpected dive. Thinking about and acting on are two very different things, however, which is why being aware of these tendencies are so important to avoid them at all costs.

This scenario happens just as frequently with trades moving in positive directions as it does negative, but the results are always going to be the same. Specifically, it can be extremely tempting to hang on to a given trade much longer than you might otherwise decide to simply because it is on a hot streak that shows no sign of stopping. In these instances, the better choice of action is to instead sell off half of your shares and then set a new target based on the updated information to ensure you are in a position to have your cake and eat it too.

Not taking your choice of broker seriously: With so many things to consider, it is easy to understand why many new option traders simply settle on the first broker that they find and go about their business from there. The fact of the matter is, however, that the broker you choose is going to be a huge part of your overall trading experience which means that the importance of choosing the right one should not be discounted if you are hoping for the best experience possible. This means that the first thing that you are going to want to do is to dig past the friendly exterior of their website and get to the meat and potatoes of what it is they truly offer. Remember, creating an eye-catching website is easy, filling it will legitimate information when you have ill intent is much more difficult.

First things first, this means looking into their history of customer service as a way of not only ensuring that they treat their customers in the right way, but also of checking to see that quality of service is where it needs to be as well. Remember, when you make a trade every second count which mean that if you need to contact your broker for help with a trade you need to know that you are going to be speaking with a person who can solve your problem as quickly as possible. The best way to ensure the customer service is up to snuff is to give them a call and see how long it takes for them to get back to you. If you wait more than a single business day, take your business elsewhere as if they are this disinterested in a new client, consider what the service is going to be like when they already have you right where they want you.

With that out the way, the next thing you will need to consider is the fees that the broker is going to charge in exchange for their services. There is very little regulation when it comes to these fees which means it is definitely going to pay to shop around. In addition to fees, it is important to consider any account minimums that are required as well as any fees having to do with withdrawing funds from the account.

Find a Mentor: When you are looking to go from causal trader to someone who trades successfully on the regular, there is only so much you can learn by yourself before you need a truly objective eye to ensure you are proceeding appropriately. This person can either be someone you know in real life, or it can take the form of one or more people online. The point is you need to find another person or two who you can bounce ideas off of and whose experience you can benefit from. Options trading doesn't need to be a solitary activity; take advantage of any community you can find.

CHAPTER 18:

Top Trader Mistakes

Options trading is an entirely different animal as compared to normal stock market investing. Let's think for a moment about the common wisdom that is dispensed with regard to stock market investing. The general idea is to buy and hold, keeping your investments for a very long period of time. In fact, basically, you're expected to keep your investments until retirement. People do various strategies such as rebalancing their portfolio to match their goals, diversification, and dollar-cost averaging.

Options trading is a totally different way of looking at things. First of all, even if you are a day trader or engaging in activities like swing trading, the general goal, when it comes to stocks, is to buy when the price is at a relatively low point, and then sell at a high price. In reality, the day trader, the swing trader, and the buy-and-hold investor are no different. Buy-and-hold investors think that they are special and above everyone else, they are in reality just trying to make money off the stock market too. The only real difference, unless you are a dividend investor, is the time frame involved. So, your buy-and-hold investor is going to hold the stocks for 25 years, and then they are going to start cashing them out for money. A swing trader makes money in the here and now.

So, in that sense of options trading is more like swing trading. And in fact, in many cases, you're looking for the same price swings that the swing trader seeks. But as we've seen, options allow many strategies that are not available for any type of stock market investor. I suppose that in theory, you could buy huge numbers of shares of stock and try to set up similar arrangements, but it just wouldn't work. And besides that, even if it did it would require an enormous amount of capital.

The point of this discussion is to just lay out the groundwork and acknowledged that most of us come to options with a completely different mindset. So does take some getting used to and many beginning options traders are going to make mistakes. That's just the nature of the market because it's so different than what people are used to.

We are going to review some of the top mistakes are made by beginning options traders. There isn't really a comprehensive list, I picked out the ones that I've noticed most people make the mistake of doing.

Going into a Trade Too Big

One of the mistakes that people make when they start out options trading is making their positions too big. Since our options don't cost all that much relative to the price for stocks, people aren't used to trading in small amounts. Even people who are not rich or anything thinking terms of the stock price and how much 100 shares with the cost. This can set up people for trouble. The temptation is going to be there to move on a large number of contracts when you start doing your trades, if you have the capital to purchase or sell them. This can actually get people into trouble. It's not really the dollar amount that's a concern, but it could get you in a position where you're not really ready to act as quickly as you might need to depend on the situation. So, if you find trade and decide to sell 20 contracts, in the event that the trade goes south trying to buyback does 20 contracts might be problematic. Or you might end up buying a bunch of call options and have trouble getting out of them on the same day. It's actually better to have a few different small positions with the options than it is to have multiple positions when they are a large number. Remember that options prices move fast. You don't want to over-leverage your trades and be in a position where you can't find a buyer to pick up all 10 or 20 contracts.

Not Paying Attention to Expiration

This is probably one of the most common mistakes made by beginning traders. The expiration date is one of the most important factors that should be considered as you enter your trades. And once you've entered a trade, you need to have the expiration date of the options tattooed on your forehead. This is something that is not amenable to being ignored. First of all, choosing the expiration date when entering the position is just as important as picking the strike price of the option. But one of the things that beginners do is to focus too much on the price of the option and the price-setting for the strike. The cost of the option and the strike price are obviously very important, the expiration date is important as well.

Unfortunately, far too many beginning traders ignore the expiration date when their trades are not working out. And so, they end up just letting the option expires. Of course, when that happens if it's out of the money, you are totally out of luck. It's just going to be at 100% loss. So, we need to be paying attention to expiration dates before we actually enter the trade, and we also need to pay attention expiration dates when we are managing the trade.

Buying Cheap Options

There is a saying that says you get what you pay for. There are reasons to buy out of the money options sometimes, but you shouldn't go too far out of the money. Unfortunately, many beginning traders are tempted to go far out of the money for the sake of buying a low-priced option. The problem with these options is that even though out of the money options can make profits. If they're too far out of the money, they simply aren't going to see any action. So, there's no sense buying a cheap option just because you can pick it up for $25. You don't want to be sinking your money into options where a massive price move would be necessary in order to earn any profits. It's fine to buy options that are near at the money. Options that are close to being in the money can be very profitable even though they are out of the money. So, if you're looking to save a little bit of money when starting out your investing, that is always something to consider. But to make profits, the basic rule is there having to be some reasonable chance that's the stock prices going to move enough, in order to make the option you purchase going the money.

Failing to Close when Selling Options

If you want to remember just one thing from our discussion about selling options, whether it's selling put credit spreads or naked puts, you should keep in mind that it's always possible to exit the trade. The way that you exit the trade when you sell to open is you buy to close. You want to be careful about doing this because it's too easy to give in to your emotions and panic and prematurely exit a trade. However, you need to be aware at all times of the possibility of needing to close the trade. Riding out an option all the way to expiration is a foolish move unless it's very clear that it's going to expire out of the money.

As a part of this problem, new options traders often come to the market and they focus on hope as a strategy. When it comes to investing, hope is definitely not a strategy. Hope is something that belongs to a casino playing slot machine games. When you're training options, you should make as rational a decision as you can make it given the circumstances. So, when the expiration date is closing and it's clear that the trade is not going to be profitable, don't give in to the temptation to say of waiting around for a reversal in direction. When you say something like that to yourself, that opens up the temptation to stay in the trade far too long. At some point, you might not be able to recover at all. So, what you don't want to do, and this is true buying and selling, is hoping that there's going to be a turnaround and waiting to see what happens.

For those who are buying options to open their positions, this is the worst of all possible strategies. Remember that when you buy to open a position, time decay is working against you at all times. So, unless the stock is moving in a good direction, there isn't a reason to hold the option. For sellers, time decay actually works in your favor. But there can be situations when it's just smart to get out of the trade. Let's look at a couple of examples.

If you sell to open an iron condor, and for some reason, the stock has a breakout to one direction or the other, it's better to get out of the iron Condor now. We aren't talking about a one- or two-dollar change. If the stock goes in such a direction that one of your options goes in the money by a small amount, that type of trade is worth waiting out to see what happens. But if there is a big break to the upside or the downside, it would be foolish to stay in the trade. For one thing, there would be at risk of assignment, but the most likely situation is that you're just going to lose the maximum amount of money. But if you have a good strategy and only getting involved with options that have a high level of open interest, almost no matter what the situation is, you should be able to buy and sell that option pretty quickly.

The other obvious example is if you were selling a put credit spread already naked put, and you noticed that the share price is declining right towards your strike price. You don't have to panic right away because remember that in order for exercising the option to be worthwhile, the share price has to move enough, so that not only does the option go in the money, but the price move also accounts for the money that was paid for the premium to buy the contract. So, if you have a strike price of $100 and someone paid two dollars to buy the option, if the share price is $99, they are going to exercise the option. Even if it drops to $98, they still might not exercise the option, unless there was some factor to indicate that the stock was about to turn around so they can sell it at a profit. But that's an unlikely scenario. It's only when it starts going strong and that there's a problem.

Trading Illiquid Options

This is such an important issue I will say it again. Liquidity is very important when trading options. What liquidity means is the ability to buy and sell financial security quickly and turn it into cash. It's not enough to like the company in order to start trading options on the company. If the open interest for an option is only 8, 10, or even 45, that is going to throw up obstacles when you need to move to get rid of an option fast. The largest companies generally have liquid options, but you should always check. Index funds also have liquid options. Avoid any companies that have small open interests. The only way that you would trade when the open interest with small is if the probability of losing out on the trade is minuscule. So, besides the strike price, share price, an expiration date, you need to be looking closely at open interest. You don't want to get in a situation where you cannot exit a position.

CHAPTER 19

5 Reasons Why Traders Lose Money

Write down these "5 Commandments" on a sticky note and put it on your computer screen:

Don't buy stocks that are hitting 52-week lows.

Don't trade penny stocks.

Don't short stocks.

Don't trade on margin.

Don't trade other people's ideas.

1. Don't buy stocks that are hitting 52-week lows.

So many new traders lose a lot of money trying to catch the proverbial "falling knife." In spite of what everyone will tell you, you are almost always much better off buying a stock that is hitting 52-week highs than one hitting 52-week lows.

Has a company that you own just reported some really bad news? If so, remember that there is never just one cockroach. Bad news comes in clusters. Many investors recently learned this the hard way with General

Electric, which just kept reporting one bad thing after another, causing the stock to crash from 30 to 7. There is no such thing as a "safe stock." Even a blue-chip stock can go down a lot if it loses its competitive advantage or the company makes bad decisions.

A cascade of bad news can often cause a stock to trend down or gap down repeatedly. If you own a stock that does this, it is often better to get out and wait a few months (or years) to reenter. Again, there is never just one cockroach.

Never buy a stock after you have seen the first cockroach. When a stock goes down a lot, it can affect the company's fundamentals as well. Employee and management morale will deteriorate, the best employees may leave the company, and it may become more difficult for the company to raise money by selling shares or issuing debt.

Conversely, when a stock goes up a lot, it can improve the company's fundamentals. Employee and management morale will be high, everyone at the company will want to work harder, it will be easier to recruit new talent, and it will become easier for the company to raise money by issuing stock or debt.

If you stick to stocks that are trading above their 200-day moving averages, or that are hitting 52-week highs, you will do much better than trying to catch falling knives.

2. Don't trade penny stocks.

A penny stock is any stock that trades under $5. Unless you are an advanced trader, you should avoid all penny stocks. I would extend this by encouraging you to also avoid all stocks priced under $10.

Even if you have a small trading account ($5,000) or less, you are better off buying fewer shares of a higher-priced stock than a lot of shares of a penny stock.

That is because low-priced stocks are most often associated with lower quality companies. As a result, they are not usually allowed to trade on the NYSE or the Nasdaq. Instead, they trade on the OTCBB ("over the counter bulletin board") or Pink Sheets, both of which have much less stringent financial reporting requirements than the major exchanges do.

Many of these companies have never made a profit. They may be frauds or shell companies that are designed solely to enrich management and other insiders. They may also include former "blue chips" that have fallen on hard times like Eastman Kodak or Lehman Brothers.

In addition, penny stocks are inherently more volatile than higher-priced stocks. Think of it this way: if a $100 stock moves $1, that is a 1% move. If a $5 stock moves $1, that is a 20% move. Many new traders underestimate the kind of emotional and financial damage that this kind of volatility can cause.

In my experience, penny stocks do not trend nearly as well as higher-priced stocks. They tend to be more mean reverting (Mean reversion occurs when a stock moves up sharply from its average trading price, only to fall right back down again to its average trading price). Many of them are eventually headed to zero, but they are still not good short candidates. Most brokers will not let you short them. And even if you do find a broker who will let you short a penny stock, how would you like to wake up to see your penny stock trading at $10 when you just shorted it at $2 a few days before? I learned that lesson the hard way. It turned out that I was risking $8 to make $2, which is not a good way to make money over the long term.

To add injury to insult, a penny stock might appear to be liquid one day, and the next day, the liquidity dries up and you are confronted by a $2 bid/ask spread. Or the bid might completely disappear. Imagine owning a stock for which there are now no buyers.

Stay away from all stocks under $10. Also stay away from trading newsletters that hawk penny stocks. The owners of these newsletters are often paid by the companies themselves to hype their stocks. Or they may take a position in a penny stock, send out an email telling everyone to buy it, and then sell their stock at a much higher price to these amateur buyers.

Watch the movie "The Wolf of Wall Street" if you'd like to see a famous example of the decadent lifestyle and fraud that often surround penny stocks. Viewer discretion is advised.

3. Don't short stocks.

If you are an advanced trader, feel free to ignore this rule. If you are not, I would seriously encourage you not to ignore this rule.

In order to short a stock, you must first borrow shares of the stock from your broker. You then sell those shares on the open market. If the stock falls in price, you will be able to buy back those shares at a lower price for a profit. If, however, the stock goes up a lot, you may be forced to buy back the shares at a much higher price and end up losing more money than you ever had in your trading account to begin with.

In November 2015, Joe Campbell broke 2 of the 5 commandments. He first decided to trade a penny stock called KaloBios Pharmaceuticals. To make things worse, he decided to short it.

When he went to bed that evening, his trading account was worth roughly $37,000. When he woke up the next morning, the stock had skyrocketed. As a result, not only had he lost all of the $37,000, but he now owed his broker an additional $106,000.

And there was no way out. If you owe your broker money, they can haul you into court and go after your house and savings.

Sometimes even the wealthiest investors can be wiped out by shorting a stock. During the great Northern Pacific Corner of 1901, shares of that railroad stock went from $170 to $1,000 in a single day. That move bankrupted some of the wealthiest Americans of the day, who had shorted the stock and were then forced to cover at higher prices.

If you do end up shorting a stock, remember that your broker will charge you a fee (usually expressed as an annual interest rate) to borrow the stock. In addition, if you are short a stock, you are responsible for paying any dividends on that stock (your broker will automatically take the money out of your account quarterly).

For all of these reasons, shorting stocks is clearly an advanced and risky trading strategy. Don't try it until you've been trading for at least 5 years, and you have the financial stability to withstand a freakish upwards move in a stock.

And never short a penny stock. It's just not worth it.

4. Don't trade on margin.

In order to short a stock, you will need to open up a margin account with your broker, as Joe Campbell did. You'll also need a margin account in order to trade stocks using margin. When you buy a stock on margin, it means that you are borrowing money from your broker, in order to purchase more shares of stock than you would normally be able to buy with just the cash sitting in your brokerage account. Let's say that I have $10,000 in my margin account. Most brokers in the U.S. will allow me to go on margin to purchase $20,000 worth of stock in that account. What this means is that they are lending me an additional $10,000 (usually at some outrageous annual interest rate like 11%, which is what E*Trade currently charges) to buy more shares of stock. If I buy $10,000 worth of stock and the stock goes up 10%, I've just made $1,000. But if I can increase the amount of stock that I'm buying to $20,000 using a margin loan, I will have made $2,000 on the same 10% move. That will mean that my trading account has just gone up by 20% ($2,000/$10,000).

Of course, if the stock goes down 10% and I'm on full margin, I will have lost 20% of my account value. Trading on margin is thus a form of leverage: it amplifies the performance of your portfolio both on the upside and the downside. When you buy a stock using margin, the stock and cash in your trading account is held as collateral for the margin loan. If the stock falls enough, you may be required to add more cash to your account immediately (this is called "getting a margin call"), or risk having the broker force you to immediately sell your stock to raise cash. Often this will lead to your selling the stock at the worst possible time. When you open up a new brokerage account and you are given the choice of a "cash account" or a "margin account," it's OK to pick "margin account." A margin account has certain advantages, such as being able to use the proceeds from selling a stock to immediately buy another stock without having to wait a few days for the trade to settle. If you never exceed your cash buying power in a margin account, you will never be charged fees or interest. In that way, it's quite possible to have a margin account, but never to go on margin.

If, however, you don't trust yourself, open up a "cash account." That way, you will never be allowed to trade on margin.

5. Don't trade other people's ideas.

There are two main reason for this.

The first reason never to trade someone else's ideas is that they probably don't know what they are doing. If you get a hot stock tip from your neighbor or at the gym, it's best to ignore it. They probably have no idea what they are talking about. Second, even if you get a really good and legitimate trading or investing idea from someone else, you will probably not have the conviction to hold on to it when the going gets tough. That conviction can only come from developing a trade idea yourself. When you have designed a trade, or researched an investment for yourself, you will have the conviction to hold on. You will also know where your stop loss is, in case the stock goes south. Have you noticed how hot stock tips never come with a recommended stop loss level?

Also, never place a trade based on something that you have just read in Barron's, Forbes, The Wall Street Journal, or have just seen on CNBC. Never buy a stock based on an analyst upgrade, or sell a stock based on an analyst downgrade.

CHAPTER 20:

Credit and Debit Spreads

Put Credit Spread

The idea behind a put credit spread is to earn money from selling a put option. But in order to mitigate the risk, you buy a put option simultaneously. This is different than selling a naked put option, where you just sell one option and that is the end of it. Since the option that you buy is going to mitigate your risk a little bit, you are not held to the same standards as someone who is selling naked put options. That said, you still have to have a level 3 trading account in order to use this strategy.

The first thing to realize about the put credit spread is that you are selling to open the position. So, this is selling, not buying to trade options. Theoretically, there is a risk of assignment, but as we'll see, it's not a real risk in practical terms, and because the trade is mitigated by the second put which you buy to open the trade, the practical impact of this is minimal.

The two options are bought and sold in one trade, so this is considered a single trade and is not two separate trades. You can buy a put debit spread, so the other party to the trade is doing that when you sell to open your position.

The belief that is behind this type of trade is that you are expecting the price of the stock to stay about where it is now, only minimally decrease in price, or increase in price. It is considered a "bullish" move, and so sometimes, goes by the name bull credit spread, but put credit spread is far more descriptive.

Second, it's not really a bullish move, in the sense that you are hoping that the stock price is going to increase by a lot. Certainly, you will be better off if that does indeed happen. If you set it up right, you will earn the maximum possible profit right off the bat and give some room for the stock to fall before that situation changes.

One of the unique properties of a put credit spread that we have not seen yet in our examination of options is that when the price reaches a certain level, that is basically it. A further increase in share price is not going to increase our profits. In the example below, consider a put credit spread for Amazon. When you sell to open the position, you get a credit to your account of $4.92 (x 100 shares for $492 total). The share price is currently in the maximum gain zone. If the share price moved up by $100, it would have zero impact on the seller of this credit spread, other than having them breathe a sigh of relief that they are definitely going to profit from the trade.

So, it's kind of a bullish strategy, but what you are really doing with a put credit spread is you are hoping that the price doesn't fall. You are using out of the money put options to set up the trade, and the hope here is that they are going to expire out of the money and that you will pocket the net premium paid on the deal.

Put Debit Spread

If you think that the stock is going down but you would rather buy to open a position, you can use a put debit spread. This is similar to a call debit spread, but in this case, you are hoping that the share price will drop. Losses are mitigated and limited to the cost to enter the position. However, profits are also capped. When you limit potential losses, you also limit potential profits.

In this case, you buy a put at a strike price that you think is going to be profitable. To lower your total risk and reduce the amount you are paying to enter the position, you sell a put option at a lower strike price.

For example, we can enter a put debit spread on Facebook with a cost to enter the position of $1.26. The higher strike price in this example is chosen to be $192.50 – we buy this put option. Then we sell a put option with a lower strike price. In this case, it's $187.50.

Maximum loss is capped at the cost required to enter the position, so we can lose $126 per contract.

Breakeven is given by the higher strike price minus the credit received, so in this case, that would be $191.24.

Maximum profit occurs when the share price drops below the lower strike price. So, the share price of Facebook would have to drop to $187.50 or below, in order to realize maximum profits.

It's possible that could happen after a bad earnings call, but it's unlikely to happen under normal circumstances without some really bad news. Of course, that does happen from time to time, but you should enter trades like this carefully, and don't do it without giving it a lot of thought and putting in some preparation. You should have a solid idea about the trade before getting into one like this.

Call Credit Spread

A call credit spread is analogous to a put credit spread, but this is a trade that you would use when you think that the stock price is going to drop. A call credit spread is a sell to open position. You make a profit by selling a call option, and you mitigate potential losses by buying a call option with the same date to end the contract date but a different strike price. In this case, you sell a call with a lower strike price. The risk is mitigated by purchasing a call with a higher strike price.

The maximum profit is the credit received from selling the position.

If the stock price goes above the lower strike price, then you are going to start losing money. To see how this works with an example, we will use Facebook. The current share price is $199.27. You can enter into a call credit spread by selling a call option with a strike price of $202.50 and buying a call option with a strike price of $210. The credit you would receive for this transaction would be $3.30, or $330 for all 100 shares. The breakeven point is easy to calculate. You do this by using the lower strike price and add it to the credit received:

$202.50 + $3.30 = $205.80.

As long as the share price stays below the lower strike price call, in this case, $202.50, the maximum profit is earned. That is the credit received or $330. Maximum loss occurs if the share prices rise above the higher strike price call, so in this case, there is a $420 loss if the share price rises above $210. Maximum loss is given by the differences in the strike prices minus the credit received. In this case:

$210 - $202.50 - $3.30 = $4.20

Call Debit Spread

A call debit spread would be an approach that is selected when you think that the share price of a stock is going to go up. In this type of scenario, you are buying a call option and selling a call option to enter into a single trade. But rather than getting a net credit the way that you do with a put credit spread, you are going to have a net debit in this case, so this is a buy to open position.

With a call debit spread, the two options have the same expiration date, and the spread comes from the options having different strike prices. In this case, you buy a call with a lower strike price. Then you sell a call with a higher strike price. You receive a credit for that, which lowers the amount that is spent on buying the lower strike price call. This will limit the amount of profit that can be made from the trade. So, the amount of profit is limited, but the risk is limited as well, since the call option that you sell will partially offset any losses you incur from the call option that you buy. The profit, in this case, is made from the call option with the lower strike price that you purchase.

The maximum loss that can be incurred buying a call debit spread is going to be given by the premium paid to enter the position.

Breakeven, in this case, is given by:

Lower call strike price + debit paid to enter the position

You pick a strike price for the lower call that you think is going to be profitable. So, you are hoping that the share price goes above this strike price. To reach the maximum profit, the share price has to reach or exceed the higher call strike price.

So, for example, we use Apple a second time. This time we are buying a call debit spread that has a lower strike price of $217.50, and a high strike price of $220. Maximum loss is incurred for any share price at expiration, which is below the bottom strike price that is $217.50. It costs $0.54 to enter the trade, so the breakeven price is $217.50 + $0.54 = $218.04. In order to make maximum profit, the share price has to go above the higher strike price, in this case, $220. The maximum gain for this trade is $196, and the most you can lose is the credit paid to enter the trade, which is $54.

To be clear, you would buy the lower strike price call – so you purchase the $217.50 call. Then you sell the higher strike price call, which means for this example, you would sell the $220 call option.

To see how the upper-priced call option lowers the cost of entry, buying the $217.50 call on its own would cost $1.64, for a total of $164. The most money than can be lost when buying a call is the price paid, so it would be $164. However, the maximum profit is theoretically unlimited.

CHAPTER 21:

How to Trade Options on
Robinhood for Beginners in 2020

What is Robinhood?

To put it simply Robinhood is an online stock brokerage app for your smartphone. Robinhood is different from other stock trading apps like E*TRADE or TDAmeritrade. The main difference is that instead of charging 5-10 dollars commission on every trade plus other fees Robinhood lets you make all your trades for free. They never charge you any commissions or fees ever. This one simple difference opens up a lot of options for everyday people that were previously only available to the rich and wealthy. Robinhood even gives away free shares of stocks like Apple, Microsoft, Ford, Sirius XM radio just for downloading their app.

When and Why to use Robinhood

Robinhood is still a new company. Using their app, you don't get the benefits of having your stocks in an IRA or Roth IRA. I wouldn't suggest using it to hold your life savings. What Robinhood is good for is starting a stock portfolio from nothing and building it with as little cost as possible to large amounts then transfer to an IRA or Roth IRA for long term benefits. In our series we are going to be using Robinhood to make more short-term trades with the goal of maximizing growth in less than 5 years.

Downloading the app and getting your first free share of stock

Robinhood will give you a free share of stock just for downloading the app and opening an account. The accounts are totally free to open so it won't cost you anything to open one. All you have to do is download the app using a referral link like this one CLICK HERE TO DOWNLOAD THE ROBINHOOD APP AND GET YOUR FIRST FREE STOCK. You will have to enter your name and information to open an account. Then look under the menu select Free Stocks. On this page you will see a link in the top right corner saying PAST INVITES click on this link to claim your free stock. You can also see a list of all the free stocks you receive here. Robinhood will give you 1 free share of a stock drawn at random from their inventory for every person you refer to using their app. You can find our techniques for getting lots of referrals (and free stocks) in the next book in our series Tons of Free Stocks on Robinhood

Watchlist and Search functions

Robinhood has a watch list just like any other stock trading platform allowing you to track the price movements of your favorite stocks. It comes preloaded with some of the most popular stocks like Facebook,

Apple, Google, and Amazon. While you can trade these stocks on Robinhood They are rather expensive anywhere from $100 to $1000. We are going to focus on using the search function to find stocks which are more affordable for beginners and adding them to our watchlist. Robinhood does not suggest stocks for you to buy and they don't have a list of all the stocks available. So, as far as finding stocks that you want to buy, you're pretty much on your own. You can search for stock tips and things like that on Google to find companies likely to go up in price and get the symbols for those companies like Facebook is FB and Apple is AAPL. Once you find the symbol for a company that you like go to the Robinhood app and click on the little magnifying glass in the top right corner. Type in the symbol you found, and you will see the company come up. From here you will see a little circle with a plus symbol inside. You can click on this symbol to add a company to your watchlist. Or, you can click on the name of the company for more details about the stock like price, volume, avg volume, market cap, dividend ratios and so forth.

Buying your first stock

By now I'm sure you're ready to get started buying and selling stock for a profit. I suggest you start small and work your way up. Find a stock you can afford and add it to your watchlist. On your watchlist click on the stock you want to buy, and the details page will come up. At the bottom of the page there is a button that will say trade or buy. Click on this button to start the buy order.

Robinhood will automatically bring up the form to place a market order. Type in how many shares you want to buy and click send. You need to be aware that when using a market order Robinhood may purchase the stock at up to a 5% higher price than current market price. In order to buy stocks at a specific price you need to use a limit order. You can change the order type by clicking on the link in the top right corner of the trading screen.

Market and Limit orders what are they used for

Basically, market orders tell Robinhood that you want to vend this stock at whatever market price is regardless of if it goes up or down. If you put in an order to buy shares Robinhood will automatically purchase available shares at up to 5% over the current market price. Anything more than 5% and it will not complete the order. Or if you place an order to sell it will sell at whatever the current market price is even if it drops rapidly.

A limit order tells Robinhood that you want to vend this stock but only if it is available at a specific price. If you use the link in the top right corner of the trading screen to change the order type to a limit order Robinhood will prompt you to enter the exact price you are about to pay for that stock and it will only complete the order if it is available at the price you enter or lower. Or if you're selling you will be prompted to enter the minimum amount your willing to vend for and it will only be completed when the price reaches that point or greater.

Stop loss and stop limit orders what are they used for

A stop loss order is an order to vend a stock if it reaches a certain price point. This type of order is your safety net and we are going to be using it a lot later in our series to minimize risk. If you switch your order type to this, you will be prompted to enter a price. If you are buying you want to enter the price you want to buy at and when the stock reaches that price or higher your order will be converted to an order. If you are selling you want to enter a price so that if the price of the stock falls below that point your order will be converted to an order. This is useful because it allows you to set up a safety net, so you don't have to be watching your stocks constantly to avoid a loss. For example, you buy a stock for $5.00. You set your stop loss order to sell if the price falls below $4.95. If the price goes up, you will continue to hold the stock and make money. If the price falls below $4.95 your order will convert to an order and sell the stock to avoid further losses.

A stop limit order is an order to vend a stock at a certain price point. But, will convert to a limit order when the stock hits that point. You must set two price points for a stop limit order. One price point at which to convert the order and another at which to limit an order. What this allows you to do is to create in which to buy the stock. For example, you think that if a certain stock breaks past its 52-week high it will get a bump from lots of people hoping it will continue to go up. But once that initial wave of buyers is over volume will go back to normal and it will go back down some then continue to rise slowly. Let's say the stock is $8 dollars per share. The 52-week high is $10 per share. You place a stop limit order with the convert price at $10 per share and the limit at $15 per share. A large hedge fund decides to buy into the stock and places a large order for millions of shares at the end of the day. The stock skyrockets to $20 in afterhours trading. You're using a free account so your orders can't execute after-market hours. In w1 the morning when the markets open the big players have already completed their orders. The price is still $20 but starts dropping because no small investors are willing to pay such a large price. Had you used a stop loss order you would have purchased the stock at a high price and then it would fall back down. But buy using a stop limit order you won't buy any shares unless the price is below $15.

CHAPTER 22

Exotic Options

An exotic option is one that has a basic structure that differs from either European or American options when it comes to the how and when of how the payout will be provided or how the option relates to the underlying asset in question. Additionally, the number of potential underlying assets is going to be much more varied and can include things like what the weather is like or how much rainfall a given area has experienced. Due to the customization options and the complexity of exotic options, they are only traded over the counter.

While they are undoubtedly more complex to get involved with, exotic options also offer up several additional advantages when compared to common options including:

They are a better choice for those with very specific needs when it comes to risk management.

They offer up a variety of unique risk dimensions when it comes to both management and trading.

173

They offer a far larger range of potential investments that can more easily meet a diverse number of portfolio's needs.

They are often cheaper than traditional options.

They also have additional drawbacks, the biggest of which is that they cannot often be priced correctly using standard pricing formulas. This may work as a benefit instead of a drawback, however, depending on if the mispricing falls in the favor of the trader or the writer. It is also important to keep in mind that the amount of risk that is taken on with exotic options is always going to be greater than with other options due to the limited liquidity each type of exotic option is going to have available. While some types are going to have markets that are fairly active, others are only going to have limited interest. Some are even what are known as dual-party transactions which mean they have no underlying liquidity and are only traded when two amiable traders can be found.

There are many different types of exotic options, including:

Choose option: The most common exotic option is known as the choose option which allows the investor in question to choose if the option is either a call or a put at different points in the option's lifetime. As this option has the ability to change during the holding period, it is not listed on any regular exchange.

Barrier option: A barrier option is an option type whose payout is going to vary depending on whether the underlying asset has reached a specific price. A barrier option may also be a knock-out at the same time which means it will expire at $0 if the underlying asset goes over a specific price as well. This then cuts into the profits of the holder but protects the assets of the writer quite nicely. On the contrary, it could also be what is known as a knock-in which means it will not have any value until the underlying asset reaches a specific price point.

Barrier options are thought of as an exotic option due to their complexity. They also come with the classification because they are a path-dependent option and their value is based on the value changes of the underlying asset during its terms of existence. Essentially this means the payoff from this type of options is based on the price path of the asset in question, not necessarily its actual price.

Asian option: An Asian option is an option that pays out based on the underlying assets average price over a set period of time as opposed to when it reaches maturity. This type of option is attractive to some traders as it can help to protect them from a period of high market volatility. It is considered an exotic option because it costs less than the standard American option.

Digital option: A digital option is a type of option with a fixed payout that will payout if the underlying stock reaches or exceeds a specific strike price. A digital option is like a binary option except that it only applies to options based on stocks specifically. If the

175

proposition upon which it is created comes to pass, then the option will be automatically exercised. They are also different from traditional binary options because they are often traded on unregulated platforms. This means that they also carry a higher overall chance of getting caught up in fraudulent activities.

Compound options: A compound option is a type of option that is created with another option as its underlying asset. This means it contains 2 different strike prices along with 2 different exercise dates. There are 4 types of compound options:

Put on a call

Call on a put

Put on a put

Call on a call

This type of option typically only appears in the fixed income or currency market where uncertainties regarding a given option's capabilities for risk protection are more prevalent. The advantages of using a compound option include large amounts of leverage at a reduced price. It is important to keep in mind that the resulting premium will still cost more than a traditional option.

Bermuda options: Bermuda options get their name from the fact that Bermuda is roughly halfway between Europe and the US. Bermuda options can be exercised at the point they expire in addition to other specific times prior to its expiration date. This type of option is useful as it provides the writer with additional control as to when the option could be exercised while also providing the buyer an alternative that costs less than the standard American option without any of the European option restriction.

Quantity-Adjusting Options: Also known as Quanto options, quantity adjusting options give a buyer access to foreign assets while still allowing them to purchase the option in their own primary currency. This option is a great choice for investors who are looking for ways to gain exposure to a new market but do not want to deal with exchange rate issues to be able to do so.

As an example, if a French investor is looking at Brazilian options due to a favorable economic situation then they may invest in the BOVESPA Index, which is Brazil's primary stock exchange. To do so without worrying about the exchange rate between the euro and the Brazilian real, they would purchase a quantity adjusting call option for the BOVESPA but denominated using euros. This lets the investor attempt to make their money as they would without worrying about getting a payout that may decrease due to unfavorable exchange rates.

Because it is essentially a two-in-one package, this option will naturally require a larger premium than average. This fact provides writers of quantity-adjusting options with additional premiums in addition to the extra risk they take on when dealing with exchange rates, so the buyers do not have to.

Look-back options: Look-back options do not have a fixed price from which they can be exercised when they are first created. Instead, the holder of these types of options is free to choose the most favorable price to exercise at any point before the option expires. These options remove all the risk associated with properly timing the entry to the market which makes them more expensive than traditional option types.

As an example, assume an investor buys into a call option with the exotic modifier of a 1-month look-back. The exercise price will then be decided once the option matures by taking the lowest price that the underlying stock ended up reaching in its lifetime. The underlying stock ends up at $106 at its expiration time, and the lowest price it achieved was $71 which means the payoff is the difference between $106 and $71 or $35.

Basket option: A basket option is very similar to a vanilla option with the exception being that they are based on more than a single underlying stock. As an example, if an option pays out based on the price of not just 1, but 3 underlying stocks then it is considered a basket option. Each underlying asset can then be worth the same amount in the end total or they can be weighted in various other quantities as well.

CHAPTER 23:

Simplified Examples of Options Trades

It is sometimes difficult for a beginner to understand options trading and the various associated terms without viewing them in the context of an actual trade.

Therefore, in here you will get to read about two different trades involving a cattle breeder and cattle traders - trades that will help you understand the connection between options trading and physical trading in the real world.

The first trade is an analogy of a typical call option trade while the second example is an analogy of a put option trade.

Once you read through these examples, you will be able to easily understand how call options and put options work. These examples should also make it easy for you to comprehend the various terms used in trading.

Trade 1: Bob's Call Option Trade

Jacob is a farmer and a cattle breeder who owns several dairy cows. Bob, who is an acquaintance of Jacob, is a trader of farm animals.

One day Bob gets a tip from a friend that the town's main dairy was negotiating a deal with a large international chocolate manufacturing company. If the deal were to materialise, the chocolate company would triple the quantity of milk they purchase from the dairy every day. To meet this increase in demand, the dairy would also have to increase milk production, and for increasing production they would have to purchase a large number of dairy cows at short notice – a move that could result in a substantial increase in cow prices locally.

Bob realised he could make some excellent profits if he bought some cows from Jacob and then sold them after the prices went up. However, Bob wasn't completely certain about this tip and did not want to buy cows upfront at the full price of $2,000 (which was the market price for a dairy cow at that time) and later sell out for a loss if the price did not rise as expected.

Therefore, Bob approaches Jacob and makes him a unique offer.

Bob tells Jacob that he will pay the latter a sum of $50 upfront for the right to buy one of his cows at the prevailing market price of $2,000, for the next 30 days. Also, Jacob would be under no obligation to return that amount if Bob no longer wanted to exercise his right (in the event that cow prices dropped below $2,000).

Jacob saw no reason for cow prices rising anytime soon and was therefore glad to sign a contract to receive $50 from trader Bob in exchange for giving Bob the right to buy a cow at $2,000 for the next 30 days.

However, Jacob puts forth a condition that the proposed contract should cover 5 cows and not just 1 cow and that meant Bob, would have to pay a total of $250 for the right to purchase 5 cows for a 30-day period.

Bob agrees to Jacob's condition and therefore, Jacob pockets Bob's $250 and then signs the contract - the contract that gave Bob the right (but not the obligation) to buy 5 of Jacob's cows at the price of $2,000 for the next 30 days.

Bob knew that in the next 30 days the market price of cows would either rise (as per his expectations), or continue to stay the same, or perhaps even fall (in the worst-case scenario).

If the market price for cows stayed the same at $2,000 or fell below that value in the next 30 days, Bob would have to simply forfeit the $250 he paid Jacob to get the agreement in place. Bob was under no obligation to buy cows at a lower price and hence his losses will be curtailed to $250 only – the money he paid Jacob to sign the contract.

On the other hand, if the market price for cows did go up within the next 30 days, Bob would approach Jacob to get 5 cows at $2,000 each and Jacob would be contractually obliged to sell the cows at $2,000, irrespective of how much more the cows were worth at that time.

Bob waits.

Three weeks after the contract was put in place, the town dairy signed a deal with the chocolate company to increase their daily supply of milk to the chocolate company by almost 4 times. To meet that demand the dairy started purchasing a large number of dairy cows at increasingly higher rates that resulted in the prices of dairy cows surging by almost 25% in the locality.

Following this price surge, Bob goes to Jacob and exercises his right to buy the 5 cows at $2,000 each. Bob then goes ahead and sells these cows to the dairy at $2,500 each.

Bob, thereby, makes a total profit of $2,250 for these 5 cows ($500 times 5 less the $250 for the contract amount he paid Jacob).

The trade that took place between Bob and Jacob is representative of how an options trade works and if we apply stock market terms into the afore-mentioned scenario then:

A single cow represents one particular underlying Share/Stock.

Bob is the Buyer of the contract and Jacob is the Seller. Since this contract gives the buyer the right to buy – this contract is a Call Option.

$2,000 represents the Market Price of the share of the given company (at the time the agreement was put in place).

$2,000 also represents the Strike-Price (SP) or the pre-determined price at which the proposed trade would take place between the buyer (Bob) and the seller (Jacob) – remember that Jacob paid $50 to purchase a cow at a fixed price of $2,000.

The $50 paid against each cow is called the Premium.

The number 5 indicates the Lot Size of the contract – it is the fixed number of shares that an individual options contract covers.

Lastly, the 30 days in this scenario denotes the Time to Expiry of the options contract.

Hope you have perfectly understood how a call option works now.

Trade 2: Jacob's Put Option Trade

After being forced to sell 5 of his cows at a price lesser than the market price due to his contractual obligation, a rather disappointed Jacob starts thinking.

From his experience, Jacob has seen that in situations where livestock prices increase sharply due to some change in the environment, the prices eventually come down marginally before reaching stability.

However, Jacob wasn't certain if cow prices had hit the ceiling yet – if he sold off his cows right away and prices continued to rise, he would miss a chance for selling at even better prices. The market price for a cow was currently at $2,500 and Jacob wanted to wait for a couple of weeks and see if it went up any further. If the prices were already at a high and if they dropped sharply, Jacob wanted to ensure that he could sell a few cows for at least $2,400.

Considering his predicament, Jacob decides to get into a contract similar to the one he had earlier signed with Bob. However, this time, he would be the 'buyer' of the right – the right to sell cows at a fixed price (unlike the right to buy that Bob purchased from him).

For this purpose, Jacob approaches Chad, a livestock trader in the local market, and offers him a deal. The deal was that, for the next 60 days, Jacob would have a right to sell Chad 10 cows at $2,400 each. And to own that right, Jacob would pay $30 per cow - a sum total of $300 for 10 cows.

Chad agrees and signs up for the deal and pockets the $300 since he didn't expect prices to fall from $2,500, let alone fall below $2,400. As long as cow prices stayed above $2,400 for the next 2 months (which Chad thought was very likely), he had nothing to lose.

A month and half later, Jacob's prediction turned out to be right and cow prices dropped down to $2,250.

Therefore, Jacob goes to Chad and exercises his right to sell the cows at $2,400.

Since Chad was contractually obliged to buy the cows at $2,400, he has no choice but to buy the cows at the fixed price despite the cows being worth $150 less in the market. Jacob thereby profits by $1200 ($150 x 10 less the $300 paid for the contract) off his trade.

Like we did last time, let's apply the various stock market terms to this trade too:

A single cow represents one particular underlying Share/Stock.

- Jacob is the Buyer of the contract while Chad is the Seller. Since this contract gives the buyer the right to sell – this contract is a Put Option.

- $2,500 - the price of the cow, represents the Market Price of a share (at the time the agreement was put in place).

- $2,400 represents the Strike-Price (SP) or the pre-determined price at which the proposed trade would take place between the Buyer (Jacob) and the Seller (Chad).

- The $30 paid against each cow is the Premium.

- The number 10 indicates the Lot Size of the contract.

- Lastly, the 60 days in this scenario denotes the Time to Expiry of the options contract.

CHAPTER 24:

When to enter and exit the trade

When you were a kid, did you ever play double Dutch jump rope? Double Dutch is where two people are swinging two ropes and a third person has to jump in for a bit before jumping out. As a kid, it was brutal and difficult to find the right timing to jump in without getting hit with a rope. Entering into a trade can be just as nerve-wracking. You can be setting up to enter the trade and stress yourself with questions like, "Do I jump in now? How about now?" But with some strategic planning, and practice, you can find the best area you would like to jump in on a regular basis.

The entry point in a trade is the point at which you want to buy an asset. It's the starting bid in your trade. Whether you are trading stocks or options, you will always have to have an entry point. Having a good plan for when you will enter into a trade is really beneficial because it means that you won't have to drive yourself mad. It also means that you won't be making an emotional choice regarding when to enter.

Choosing a good entry point means analyzing the chart for support, resistance, and trend. Look at the past movement of the chart and find the support and resistance. Then, look at the trend. Has the chart been moving in a specific trend line? Or has it been in a stage of consolidation? Or a period where the market has remained fairly steady? With a stock that has a trend line, you can choose a point right after a rebound. For example, let's say stock ABC was trading at $60 in November before dropping to $58. As the number starts to rise again, you can see if the chart seems like it's going to return to trend. If yes, then you can place your entry point at $60 and wait to see if the trend will continue upward.

In the case of a stock that is at a stage of neutral movement, then your support and resistance lines will be horizontal, and the chart will remain between those two lines. In this case, follow the pattern of the previous movement and again place your entry point at the price where a rebound is likely to happen. This should be close to the support line. There's a good chance that the stock value will rise again towards the resistance in this case.

Let's put this into action. Chose two different practice charts. One should have a stock that is trending upwards, and one should have stock that is steady and isn't trending in a particular direction. Taking the one that is trending upward, draw the trend line in the support line position. From there, choose a position that offers you a small swing up. At what point would you enter the swing? At what price point? How long would you remain in the swing? Do the same for the chart that is remaining steady. What point above the support line would you enter into the trade? It's easy to do this with past charts because everything is already lined up. But take the time to analyze the chart. What makes specific swings more successful and what makes them unsuccessful?

Now try with a practice future trade. Again, find a chart from a stock that you would be interested in purchasing. Map out your lines, find the zone you'll trade in, and then choose an entry point either in the present or the future. After that, watch the stock for the next several days. Would your trade have panned out? If yes, why? And if no, why not? All of this practice gives you the opportunity to try out trades before investing any capital into it. Once you feel a bit more confident about entry points, move on to learn about exit points.

When you enter into the trade, you need to make sure that your risk/reward ratio makes the trade worth it. Once you calculate the ratio, you can determine at what point you can exit the trade in order to make the reward worth it.

Now we're going to learn how to exit a trade. It is very important to have an exit strategy. Without an exit strategy, you will choose to leave a trade whenever you feel like it, which can cause you some losses. You may exit too early or too late. It is better to have a strategy in place so that you know exactly when you'll exit. For example, if you determine that you would like to make a specific amount of profit, that's your exit point. Don't go past that.

As you throw it, momentum keeps it going higher but at a slower pace until it reaches its peak. At this point, momentum is zero and the ball falls back to your hands. In a swing trade, you want to exit the trade before the momentum reaches zero. Not at the peak, but before the peak. This is because most traders will be looking to sell at the peak of the trade, which will cause a drop in the market. Selling early before the estimated peak is a risk. It might mean that you lose out if the ball continues to go much higher than you anticipated. However, you will still have made a gain before any reversal happens and you can always buy back into the trend if you want to.

When looking at the charts for a stock, you should keep in mind your entry position and where you would like to exit. If the stock has stayed steady over the last bit of time and remains in its range, then looking at the support and resistance can give you a good idea of where to exit. If you entered near the support, then you can determine at what point you would like to exit. This depends on a lot of factors like your tolerance for risk and how long you want to stay in the trade. Generally speaking, if the stock value keeps increasing, you want to exit before it hits the resistance. Remember, in swing trading, it's all about small gains, not large ones so it's better to leave with some profit rather than no profit.

• With your support and resistance marked on a chart, you can also look for key indicators that show you that it's time to sell. One of these indicators is either if the stock value exceeds its resistance, or if it drops below its support numbers. This can mean that it's starting to trend in one specific direction, but it could also mean that these little breakouts will backtrack into the range it was sitting at before. If the stock value exceeds its resistance and you haven't sold yet, then you can choose to wait until it returns to its range or see if it will be the start of a new trend. This decision, again, depends on how much risk you're willing to take.

There are a couple of things you can do to make sure that you are not staying in a trade too long. The first one is to set a stop-loss. A stop-loss is a tool that will sell your shares in the event that the stock price goes too low. The other option is to set a limit order. A limit order will sell your trades once they've reached your set peak value. Let's say that the current stock price for ABC is $20 per share when you enter. You can choose to set your limit order at $25 a share. You can also set it at a certain percentage point for profit. This means that at the $25 mark, your broker will sell your shares. This can be good because it can limit your losses, but it can also prevent you from taking advantage of a possible trend. So once again, make a decision based on your tolerance for risk.

As you make your exit strategy, you should ask yourself a few questions. You should know how long you are willing to stay in a trade, how much risk you can tolerate and at what point you want to get out. These three things will help you make a good exit strategy. For example, when asking yourself how long you want to stay in a trade, you can think about how long you want your capital to be tied up, what indicators you're looking for that will cause you to sell, etc.

When considering how much risk you're willing to take, try a few different scenarios. Also, consider what a profit is to you. Is it a $1 per share a decent profit or do you want to make more? Finally, consider when you want to leave the trade. You should have this written down clearly. Are you going to leave the trade once you've made a certain profit, once you hit the resistance level, or once you see another indication that it's time to go? When you've made your plan, it's important you stick to it. This will help you remain emotionally objective when trading.

Once you've made your exit plan, it's time again to practice. Look at some past charts and analyze where you would have entered and exited the trade, based on the indicators like support and resistance, or based on the moving average. Analyze every piece of a move. Why would a certain exit point have worked or failed? Afterwards, try this again with a future chart. You can either do this in a simulation or using your own chart website of choice. Pick a stock you want to follow and find an entry point you think will work for you. Then, using your exit strategy, determine when you will exit the chart. Spend a few days looking at your plan as the chart moves forward. Did your plan work? Are there other ways you could have executed it? Keep practicing, don't just do this with one chart and think you're ready to start trading.

Where to place your stop-loss and why

We've talked a little about stop-losses, but let's look at them in more detail and explore the different types you can use. A stop-loss is very similar to a fire alarm. The fire alarm in your house starts to go off the moment that it senses smoke. It doesn't have to be a literal fire for it to sound the alarm. This can be kind of irritating, but it is also a very close analogy of what a stop-loss is. And yes, on occasion a stop-loss can also be irritating if it's not set correctly. A stop-loss can help you sell your trades when the market turns in an unexpected direction. It's your warning system and safety net in one. It makes sure that if the market is going to drop, you aren't going to lose a massive amount of money. However, sometimes a stop-loss is placed too tight which results in it being triggered during regular market volatility. This is that annoying accidental fire alarm. Even though it can be annoying, a stop-loss can save you considerable grief. As a swing trader, your trades will cover some days and weekends, which can result in precarious nights where the market shifts unexpectedly. A stop-loss can help you ensure your losses aren't too steep.

CHAPTER 25:

Financial Leverage

To use leverage, you have to make use of various instruments, including future, options, and margin accounts.

The use of leverage n options trading helps boost your profits. Trading in options can give you huge leverage and allow you to generate huge profits from a small investment.

Definition

Leverage is the ability to trade a large number of options using just a small amount of capital. Many traders feel that leverage is, but studies have found that the risk in leveraged options is nearly the same to non-leveraged securities.

Why Is Leverage Riskier?

Trading options using leverage is usually considered riskier because it exaggerates the potential of the business. For instance, you can use $500 to enter a trade that has a potential of $7000. Remember the first rule of trading – don't trade what you cannot lose.

This isn't as true as it seems, which is why it is vital that you know what you are doing at all times.

Leverage makes you utilize capital more efficiently. For this reason, many traders love the trade because it allows them to go for larger positions with limited capital.

When you use leverage, you don't reduce the potential profit that you will gain; rather, you reduce the risk in certain trades. For instance, if you want to put your money in 10,000 options at $8 per share, you will need to risk $80,000 worth of investment. This means that the whole amount of $80,000 would be at risk. However, you can use leverage to place a smaller amount of money, thus reducing the risk of loss.

This is the way you need to look at leverage, which is the right way.

Before you can trade leverage, you need to find a way to maximize the gains in each trade.

Here are a few tips that you can explore:

Know When to Run

You need to cut losses early enough and then let your winning trades run to completion. Just the way you run other trades; you need to know when to cut your losses so that you don't end up bankrupt. You need to make use of stop losses when running leverage in trades.

Have a Stop Loss Set?

As a trader, you need to determine your stop loss set so that you don't lose more than you can afford. The set that you come up with will depend upon the situation of the market at any time. Whatever the case, always make sure you have a set to guide you.

Don't Go with the Trade

Many traders try to chase a trade to the finish, something that ends up discouraging them and making them lose money. Once a move happens, you need to accept and wait for the next opening. Always be patient because just like the other opportunity came along, another one will definitely come by.

Have Limit Orders

Instead of placing market limits, opt for limit orders instead so that you can save on fees. The limit orders also help you reign in your emotions when you trade.

Learn About Technical Analysis

Make sure you learn about technical analysis before you jump into trading. Technical analysis will make sure you have the information that you need to make decisions fast.

The Advantages of Leverage in Options Trading

When you use leverage, you increase your financial capability as a trader and enjoy better trading results. You can change the amount of leverage at your discretion. This is because when you open a trading account, you have all the power of managing the amount of capital that you place on a trade. The good news is that you can use leverage free of charge, but you need to make sure you know how it works and whether it will work for you or not.

The level of leverage varies. Some trading platforms offer leverage from as low as 1:1 up to and beyond 1:1000. As a trader, it is advisable that you go for the largest leverage possible so that you can make the biggest returns.

Another advantage is that low leverage allows you as a new trader to survive. When starting out in options trading, you have the capacity to make small trades with little to show for your efforts. With leverage, you can make use of leverage to place trades that run into thousands of dollars without risking the same amount in terms of investment. As long as you know what you are doing, you have the capability to enjoy massive profits.

Disadvantages of Leverage in Options Trading

As much as it is a good way to make huge profits, you also need to understand that leverage comes with many demerits. These include:

Magnifies the Losses

With leverage, you will be faced with huge losses if the trade decides to go the other way. And since the original outlay is way smaller than what you end up losing, many traders forget that they are placing their capital at risk. Make sure you come up with a ratio that will help protect your interests and then know how to manage trade risk.

No Privileges

When you use leverage to trade, you sacrifice full ownership of the asset. For instance, when you use leverage, you give up the opportunity of enjoying dividends. This is because the amount on the dividend is deducted from the account regardless of the position of the trade.

Margin Calls

A margin call is when the lender asks you to add funds so that you keep the trade open. You have to decide whether you wish to add funds or exit a position to reduce the exposure.

Incur Expenses

When you use leverage to trade options, you will receive the money from the lender so that you can use the full position. Most traders opt to keep their positions open overnight, which attracts a fee to cover the costs.

How Much Leverage Do You Need in Options Trading?

Knowing how to trade options needs detailed knowledge about the various aspects of economics. For many people, the lack of knowledge to use leverage is the major cause of losses.

Studies show that many traders who opt for options lose money in the process. This happens whether for smaller or high leverage.

Risks of High Leverage

In options trading, the capital for placing a trade is usually sourced from a broker. While you have the ability to borrow huge amounts to place on a trade, you can gain more if the trade is successful.

A few years back, traders were able to offer leverages of up to 400 times the initial capital. However, rules and regulations have been, and at the moment, you can only access 50 times what you have. For instance, if you have $1000, you can control up to $50,000.

Choosing the Right Leverage

You need to look at different factors when choosing the kind of leverage that will work for you.

First, you need to start with low levels of leverage, because the more you borrow, the more you will need to pay back. Second, you need to use stops to make sure you protect the amount you have borrowed. Remember losses won't go down well with you.

All in all, you need to choose leverage which you find is comfortable for you. If you are a beginner, go for low leverage so that you minimize risks. If you know what you are doing, then go for maximum leverage to build your returns.

Using stops on order allows you to reduce loses when the trade changes direction. As a newbie, this is the only protection you need to make it in the market. This is because you will learn about the trades and how to place them while limiting any losses that might arise.

How to Manage Risk in Options Trading

Options trading comes with a number of risks that you need to manage so that you can enjoy the profits and minimize losses.

Here are a few risks and how to deal with them.

Losing More than What You Have

This risk is inherent in options trading, especially if you are using leverage to make a trade. It means that you put up a small fraction of the initial deposit to open the trade. This means that your fate is in the hands of the direction of the market. If it goes along with your prediction, you will gain more than the deposit. On the other hand, if the direction changes and you lose the position, you might end up losing more than your initial deposit.

When this happens, you need to have a strategy in place to help mitigate the risk. What you need to do in this case is to set a limit, so that you define the exact level at which the trade should stop so that you don't lose more than you can handle.

Positions Closing Unexpectedly

When positions close unexpectedly, they lead to loss of money. To keep the trades open, you need to have some money in the account. This aspect is called the margin, and if you don't have enough funds to cover the margin, then the position might close.

To mitigate this, you need to keep an eye on the running balances and always add funds as needed.

Sudden Huge Losses or Gains

The market can turn out to be volatile, and when it does, you need to move fast. Markets change depending on the news or something else in the market, which can be an announcement, event, or changes in trader behavior.

Apart from having stops, you also need to get notifications regarding any upcoming movement, which tells you whether to react or not,

Orders Filled in Erroneously

When you give instructions to a broker to place a trade for you, and the broker instead does the opposite. This is termed slippage. When this happens, use guaranteed stops to make sure you protect yourself against any slippage that might occur.

How to Trade Smarter Using Leverage

Even with leverage in tow, you need to have a way to trade better. With many mistakes occurring during a trade, you stand to lose more than gain if you don't have the right tips to excel. Let us look at the top mistakes that you go through to get to the top.

Misunderstanding Leverage

Many beginners don't understand leverage and go ahead to misuse this feature, barely realizing the risk they are exposing themselves to.

To make this work for you, learn about leverage, and master it. Understand what it is and what it isn't and then find out the best ways to make use of it. You also need to understand how much you can put in without running huge losses.

Having No Exit Plan

Just like socks, you need to control your emotions when trading options. It doesn't mean that you have to swallow your greed and fear; rather, you need to have a plan that you can go with. Once you have a plan, you need to stick to it so that even when things aren't going your way, you have something to guide you to make a recovery.

You need to have an exit plan, which means you know when to drop a trade.

Failure to Try New Strategies

You need to make sure you try out a few new strategies depending on the level of trading you want to achieve. Most traders get a single strategy and then stick to it even when it is not working out for them. When this happens, you are often tempted to go against the rules that you set down.

Maintain an open mind so that you can learn new option trading strategies to help you get more out of your trades.

CHAPTER 26:

Moneyness

The term moneyness is used in Options trading to describe the financial status of an Option. An option is said to be in the money— or profitable to exercise if its strike price is lower than the price of the underlying asset. For example, it would be in the money if you could exercise your rights to buy the underlying stock at the strike price to immediately sell on the market for a profit.

However, the concept of moneyness has a few different aspects to it.

Remember that the strike price is the locked-in price that the underlying stock can be bought or sold for, if exercised. Therefore, the strike price is an important factor in determining the Options value as we can compare the Options strike price with the actual market price of the stock. This relationship between the strike and actual market price determines the intrinsic value of the Option and will be a determining factor:

At the money: This is when the strike price and the stock price is the same and so it applies to both calls and puts

Near the money: As it is unlikely for the strike and actual price to exactly match any close to equality is termed near the money

In the money: This is when the strike price in a call option is below the price of the actual stock. On the other hand, with a put option, the strike price is in the money when it is above the stock price

Out of the money: This is when a call option strike price is above the stock price. With a put option, the strike price will be out of the money when it is below the stock price

As you start to practice and gain experience working with quote tables and orders, you will become very familiar with these terms. This is because you will soon become accustomed to using the relationship between the stock price and the strike price to determine if there is any intrinsic value in the Option. A thing to remember is that only options that are "in the money" will have any intrinsic value.

Indeed, an option will be said to be in the money only if it is profitable to exercise. It is out of the money if it is not profitable. This means that just because the strike price is above or below the actual price doesn't automatically make it in the money as we must always consider the cost of the premium. Also, the relationship of the underlying price to the strike price depends on the type of option involved.

In other words, a long call is in the money if the strike price is less than the underlying stock price. Therefore, you would make a profit if you to exercise your rights under the option, by buying the underlying asset, and then selling it at the higher market price. On the other hand, if the underlying stock price is less than the strike price, then the option is out of the money.

Conversely for the writer of the option, the trader that is obliged to fulfill the holder's rights whether that is to buy or to sell, then they will have the opposite point of view. For the writer of the Option has taken a short position and will be out of the money when the price of the underlying asset is greater than the strike price and in the money when the price of the underlying asset is less than the exercise.

Similarly, the positions are reversed when we consider relative perspectives of the holder and writer of the put option. For example, if the holder of a put option has a strike price of $35 and if the underlying stock is trading at more than $35, then they would be out of the money as it would not be profitable to exercise, so the long put position would be out of the money. However, the holders long put would be in the money if the underlying were to trade at less than $35.

But conversely, if we consider the short put position, we will find that an underlying price of more than $35 would mean the option would not be exercised by the holder, so the writer could keep the premium and be in the money. But, if the underlying stock price were to fall below $35, then the option would be in the money from the holder's perspective as it could be exercised at a profit and the writer's short position would now be out of the money.

The following table offers a neat summary of it all.

The Moneyness of an Option

Position	In the Money	Out of the Money
Long call	Stock > Strike	Stock < Strike
Short call	Stock < Strike	Stock > Strike
Long put	Stock < Strike	Stock > Strike
Short put	Stock > Strike	Stock < Strike

Stock = current market price of the underlying stock (variable)

Strike = the locked-in strike price of the Option (fixed)

As we can see the holder and the writer of the Options always have an opposite position except when the strike price and the underlying price are the same, then the option is at the money or near the money. This is regardless of the type of option whether it is a put or a call, or whether you are going long or short.

Furthermore, the moneyness of an option is not affected by the style of the option. What this means is that even with a European option, which can only be exercised at the expiry time, it can still transition many times during that period often jumping between being in, out, or at the money at any given time.

Open Interest

An interesting metric that is often included in quote tables for Option contracts is an indicator depicting Open interest, which is the total number of outstanding options contracts. Open interest is tallied at the end of each day. Open interest is used as a metric for the measurement of market sentiment. It should not be misinterpreted as the number of options traded because it is not the same thing as volume as many options are traded to close out existing positions.

However, if you are speculating in short term trading of options then Open Interest is an important metric as you will want as much market interest as you can get on your option. This will make it easier to trade when you choose to exit the position as there will likely be many potential buyers.

Expiration and Exercise

Options expire at regular intervals determined by the expiration date, which is the date the option expires. Most options expire on the third Friday of a given month. However, some high-volume weekly options have expiration dates every Friday. The last time to trade the option is at the close of the market immediately before the option expires. Some European options close earlier (sometimes on a Thursday but the closing time would be specified for the option, and most broker apps track the options expiry dates and send a notification, so you'd know):

The option period is the term used to denote the valid time until expiration and it starts the moment the option is made (written) and ends on the expiry day. However, there are ways to stay in the position if you want to beyond the expiry date. If you want to maintain the position you can roll by closing your current – soon to expire - open position and simultaneously make a new position at a different strike price or expiration.

Weighing Option Costs and Benefits

There are many advantages to trading using options, but you don't get all those benefits without taking on-board some element of risk. A notable risk that you have to accept is that options have a limited lifespan as they are limited by expiry date. Now there are clear strategies that you must have in place when handling this risk such as having an exit strategy. For example, your choices are, trade the option during the timespan of the option, expire the option on or before the expiry date or simply let the option expire.

However, there can be a big problem with just leaving options to expire. For example, if the option is in-the-money at expiration, your broker may well automatically exercise/assign the option. The problem here is that by exercising the valuable option they have effectively converted a low-cost option position into a high-cost stock position, which you may not want or be able to afford. Consequently, you need to carefully monitor your options and check for notifications from the broker platform regarding any in-the-money option positions, which are nearing the expiration date. You need to do this in anticipation of this likely change in your margin requirement. Alternatively, you want to make sure you have sufficient time to trade the option or make other adjustments such as rolling over a trade in order to avoid buying the stock.

Risk of Leverage

Another significant risk to be aware of is that of leverage. Because Options don't cost much as stock as they are simply a contract, this means that they experience disproportionately larger percentage price gains in reaction to the far more expensive underlying stock's very small price movements. The huge benefit of this is that it results in large percentage gains when the underlying stock moves in the anticipated direction by even a small amount. The downside though is that it also results in a 100% wipe-out of the investment if the stock moves by even the smallest amount in the wrong direction. This is not necessarily an issue with beginners or at least it shouldn't be as the risk manifests itself mainly through trading too large a position size. However, you need to be aware that as beneficial as leverage clearly is, it can also be a double edge sword, so be aware that leverage is a risk that needs to be addressed. One simple way to nullify or minimize this level of risk is to keep your position size small.

Lastly, Options, as we know, possess a time value (extrinsic value) in addition to their inherent intrinsic value (in the money value), which is also another double-edged sword. For option buyers, time-decay acts as a headwind because it is continually decreasing the value of the option. By doing so this increases the dependency on greater stock price movement to break even on the trade. For option writers, it acts as a tailwind because it allows a profit to be generated through steady premium incomes regardless of whether the stock moves or not.

Two other option cost factors should be considered:

Costs associated with the trading process

Cost of exercising the stock

By understanding the basic cost structure for an option, you can see how options also add through leverage an element of risk, despite the fact that options also provide leverage at a reduced risk.

To complicate the matter a little is the fact that Option prices are partially based on probabilities. For stock options, you want to consider the likelihood that a particular option will be in-the-money before or at expiration given the type of price movements the underlying stock has recently undergone.

The way an Option is valued takes into consideration 6 factors; Stock price, strike price, time to expiration, interest rates, and dividends but there is a wildcard factor – volatility.

Conclusion

One of the leading ways of gaining financial freedom is setting up passive income streams. Trading options has the potential to be a powerful form of passive income. Not only does this activity give the trader the platform to gain financial freedom but it also allows the trader to pursue hobbies, career options and other activities that he or she loves. It allows this because the trader is not actively trading time for money. Options traders have the flexibility to live and work anywhere in the world because, when done right, trading options allows the trader to earn tens of thousands of dollars and more even while he or she sleeps.

This book was written as a comprehensive guide to show that any and every one can earn a sizable income from options trading as long as this person is willing to develop a growth mindset, learn from the mistakes and successes of other traders and work to put in that human and financial investment upfront. Options are derivative contracts that allow the owner of the contract the right to buy or sell the associated asset by an expiration date specified. From this definition, you can see that this is not something you simply dabble in every now and then.

Are You Ready to Be an Options Trader?

Trading options is a business. Therefore, it needs to be approached with a mindset that is set for growth and development. We have talked about many topics on how you can get started such as developing your training plan, paper trading, opening a brokerage account and choosing a trading style. All of these things plus learning the language of options trading is greatly important as a beginner in this field. You cannot get through into this career and profit in the way that you would like without putting in that initial study.

After you have done this, you need to practically implement the strategies and techniques taught in this book. To remember what a put option and a call option are, you need to be able to see them in practice. To mentally solidify what a long position and a short position are, you need to actually be in these positions. To become familiar with volatility and interest rates, you need to put yourself in a position to learn further. Straddles, strangles, legging, debit spreads, credit spreads, selling naked options and rolling out options... They might seem intimidating on paper and might be difficult to implement at first, but practice makes perfect. All advanced options traders started as a beginner, but consistent, persistent effort took them to the next level.

This is a new world for any novice and, of course, it can seem intimidating but as long as you remained committed to developing the traits of a successful options trader, you will be well on your way to

217

obtaining the financial freedom that you crave. Just as with any new venture, there will be setbacks and failures. You will lose your footing sometimes and be exposed to things that you never have been before.

CPSIA information can be obtained
at www.ICGtesting.com
Printed in the USA
BVHW050712230721
612633BV00012B/606